THE
PROGRESSIVE
YEARS

AMERICA COMES OF AGE

Irwin Unger

NEW YORK UNIVERSITY
CONSULTING EDITOR

THE PROGRESSIVE YEARS

AMERICA COMES OF AGE

William L. O'Neill

RUTGERS UNIVERSITY

DODD, MEAD & COMPANY

New York   1975

To Merle Curti

Library of Congress Catalog Card Number: 74-26163
ISBN: 0-396-07101-5
PRINTED IN THE UNITED STATES OF AMERICA

EDITOR'S
INTRODUCTION

The progressive period is a challenging one to a student of American history. Coming at the beginning of the twentieth century, it represents in an obviously chronological way the beginning of modern times. It also represents the launching point for many of the events that crowd the daily newspapers today and color our lives.

If we think about it we can see in how many ways the years from 1900 to 1917 presage the 1970s. Our own era, for instance, has been characterized as the "automobile age." By 1916 there were three and a third million automobiles registered in the United States. Our era has also been referred to as the "age of the city." By 1910 forty-two million Americans lived in urban communities (2,500 or more), just under half the total population. (By the next census, more than half lived in urban communities.) Modern America has been described as a "welfare state." The roots of the welfare legislation that has transformed the quality of American life go back to the political reforms adopted or proposed by the progressives before World War I.

Clearly the progressive period is relevant to men and women living in the 1970s. And yet progressivism and the people who fought for it have not always been praised by historians, biographers, and journalists. Perhaps if Americans were happier with their own times, they might like the progressives more. Unfortunately, much of the promise of American life seems to have been unfulfilled, and we find it hard not to hold the men and women of the first years of the century at least partially responsible for getting our hopes up.

Yet, this is an unfair judgment. Seldom in any generation has America produced a more interesting, more intelligent, more alert, more sympathetic group of men and women in every walk of life. The United States came to maturity in the progressive period, and the country's cultural, political, and intellectual life then was interesting, sophisticated, and creative as never before. It was during these years that American civilization, in all its aspects, developed a density and a subtlety of texture that deserved comparison with the best that Europe had to offer.

This growing complexity and subtlety make the period controversial and difficult to interpret. In an earlier day most historians praised the progressives for their democratic sympathies and for their efforts—only partially successful, admittedly—to tame the forces of unchecked acquisitiveness and to improve the lot and well-being of the average citizen. Most certainly scholars of the 1920s and 1930s never doubted that there was a complex but reasonably coherent group of men with similar ideas who could be labeled "progressives." But following World War II, the scholarly picture changed. By then progressive reformers of all sorts were suspect. Often they were judged to have been crankish, egocentric, or paranoid. Their outward intentions were above reproach perhaps, but they appeared to have acted more out of personal anxieties or uncertain social status than out of love or compassion. Middle-class professionals and small businessmen, for the most part, they were seen to have universalized their own feelings (and biases) and claimed more humanity and social benevolence for their cause than it rightly deserved.

Still later, in the 1960s, a number of scholars attacked the progressives as agents of big business intent on holding off socialism or true democratic reform by the use of sophisticated subterfuge and subtle deception. Countering this charge was that of another school of historians who accepted the sincerity of the progressives, but added to the interpretive confusion by insisting that many of the supporters of the progressives were really urban working-class folk, who had adopted and reinforced the social welfare and good government program of the progressives. Indeed, sometimes they even did

this through the urban political machines that in traditional progressive historiography were among the chief targets of progressive
reformers! By now, in the 1970s, the picture is so confused that one
young American historian has seriously proposed to chuck out the
whole concept of progressivism as a meaningless convention.

Obviously it is not William O'Neill's belief that there was no such
thing as progressivism. However, he is not willing to take the progressives at their own self-evaluation. They were often sanctimoni-
ous and often self-deceived. Still more to the point, they were often
inadequate to the tasks that they set themselves. And yet, as O'Neill
shows, the era in which they lived and performed was full of new
beginnings and intellectual and political excitement. In witty, supple
prose that eminently fits the nature of his subject, he gives us a
compelling and entertaining portrait of an age and a movement.

IRWIN UNGER

PREFACE

To the political and social activists who lived through it the Progressive era, which began around 1900 and lasted until about 1918, seemed a great age of reform. They saw it as a time when monopolists and plutocrats were restrained, political machines destroyed, government on every level was made more democratic and responsive, and the fight for social justice pushed forward. Many historians have taken the same general view, but in the 1960s a number concluded that the age was really a time when middle-class people and big businessmen enhanced their own interests, sometimes by disguising self-serving acts as reforms. Gabriel Kolko calls his influential study of business regulations during the years 1900–16 *The Triumph of Conservatism*. Robert H. Wiebe in his *The Search for Order, 1877–1920* argues forcefully that this period witnessed the rise of a new, bureaucratically oriented middle class. To his mind progressivism was not a struggle between the "people" and the "interests," as used to be said, but was instead the replacement of outdated values with new ones held by the new middle class, particularly values of "continuity and regularity, functionality and rationality, administration and management."

In writing this book I have drawn heavily on the new scholarship that is critical of progressivism and the Progressive era. At the same time I have qualified its judgments rather sharply at points, and many of the authors whose works are cited in my bibliographical notes will not agree with what is written here. For one thing, I feel that radical historians in particular have a tendency to portray leaders such as Theodore Roosevelt and Woodrow Wilson as more consistently ideological than politicians can afford to be. I also think that businessmen have been given more credit for vision and far-sightedness than they deserve. Very few people, even powerful and intelligent ones, can read the future clearly. Nearly everyone involved in making important decisions has a short-term frame of reference; luck and accident as well as planning shape events; actions sometimes have unintended consequences.

Nevertheless, the new scholarship has helped me to see the Progressive era more as an age of modernization than of reform. Reformers were plentiful, and significant steps were taken locally and nationally to promote the general welfare. But it became clear in later years that the principal beneficiaries of the era were middle- and upper-class people. Better government in many cases meant government that was more efficient and responsive to their needs. As we shall see, other groups made gains too, but not on the same scale. This history of the Progressive era, therefore, is the story of how after many battles and much confusion, the basis was laid for the bureaucratized, business-dominated, limited welfare state we live in now. [A masterful essay reviewing and analyzing the literature on this period is Robert H. Wiebe, "The Progressive Years, 1900–1917," in William H. Cartwright and Richard L. Watson, Jr., eds., *The Reinterpretation of American History and Culture* (1973).]

A word on terms might be useful here. As with all political labels, "progressive" has meant different things to different people. It came into general use around the turn of the century to apply to any person or proposal that today would be called "liberal." Since the term was so broad, embracing all sorts of people from social reformers to big businessmen, there is probably no excuse for using it except that it was the word favored at the time. It was most often used by people who were neither radical nor conservative to describe themselves. I have tried to make clear as I go along what the term means in the case of important individuals and groups, but its indiscriminate use by contemporaries makes precision difficult. Readers who find themselves confused on the point should be comforted by the knowledge that almost everyone is. When "Progressive" is capitalized in this text it applies strictly to the Progressive party of 1912–16 and its members, or to the era as a whole. After 1916 "progressive" had acquired a partisan character because of its use by the Progressive party and thereafter "liberal" gradually replaced it.

A number of scholars have read the manuscript and saved me from numerous errors and infelicities. I would like to thank especially Irwin Unger of New York University, Stanley K. Schultz of the University of Wisconsin, and David P. Thelen of the University of Missouri. I am particularly grateful for the opportunity to dedicate this book to Merle Curti, a former colleague and admired friend. Like many in our profession I have benefited from his kindness and courtesy, and been inspired by his great achievements both as a scholar and a human being. The study of American history owes much to him and so also do its students. I hope he will take this as a small payment on a very large debt.

WILLIAM L. O'NEILL

CONTENTS

1

ORIGINS OF
THE PROGRESSIVE ERA

For most of its history what is now the United States has been an underpopulated country, made up largely of farmers. Until about a century ago business enterprises were small, few in number, and locally oriented. There was no national market economy, and only a handful of importers and producers of commodities and raw materials were involved in foreign trade. Growth meant chiefly opening up new farmlands. As time went on all these conditions changed. The urban population began to grow more rapidly than the rural. Manufacturing became as important as agriculture. By the 1890s most of the best arable land had been taken up. Thereafter agricultural growth depended more on the intensive farming of existing land than on acquiring new holdings. This took larger and larger sums of money, as did the growing businesses and industries of urban America. The capitalist system came to dominate the working lives of most Americans. Improved means of transportation —especially the railroad—created a national market economy, binding the scattered peoples of a vast continental state together for the first time.

In the long run increased productivity in business, manufacturing, and agriculture benefited the American people greatly. But in the short run the changes required to accomplish this often seemed to create more problems than they solved. A nation of subsistence farmers had little to fear from market crashes and depressions. On the other hand, a nation of shopkeepers, industrial workers, commodity growers, and clerks was increasingly vulnerable to economic downturns. Unemployment was a constant threat to the new proletariat created by industrialization and to the army of salaried white-collar workers as well. Bankruptcy haunted the dreams of businessmen operating in an unstable environment where bust followed boom with alarming frequency. Commodity growers, unlike subsistence farmers, were at the mercy of world markets, whose workings were mysterious and remote. Thus, while Victorian America was prosperous, nearly all the great population blocs —farmers, big businessmen, the new technicians and bureaucrats, tradesmen, the old professional classes, the new proletariat—were dissatisfied. Their unhappiness was crystallized by the economic crisis of the 1890s, which became, like the depression of the 1930s, one of those great, transforming experiences that would shape the nation for years to come.

BACKGROUND FOR THE CRISIS

Even before the crisis thoughtful Americans suspected that existing nineteenth-century guides to policy making were inadequate. The common view was that government should be limited, putting no impediments in the way of enterprise and liberty, but granting no special favors either. In practice, however, government was both weak and discriminatory. Ship owners, railroaders, users of the public domain sang hymns to laissez-faire (government nonintervention), even as they lobbied government and used the courts to advance their private interests. As time went on the contradiction between what government was supposed to do and what it was actually doing became more obvious and less tolerable.

Another nineteenth-century belief that suffered from contradictions was the idea of competition. Competition was held to be the instrument through which progress manifested itself. Darwin was misread by people who used his ideas to argue that evolution, social as well as biological, was the product of ceaseless struggle. The fittest—that is to say, the strong—must prosper; the weak, by definition unfit, must fail. But while most Americans believed in competition, few were willing to accept this logical conclusion. Humanitarian and philanthropic activities grew after the Civil War, even though they enabled the unfit to survive. Public schools expanded rapidly, even though public education supposedly allowed all children, regardless of parental merit, to enjoy equal advantages. Competition was further undermined by protective tariffs which allowed American manufacturers to charge higher prices than would have been possible in a free market. And competition was weakened still more by business combinations that formed, or tried to form, trusts and monopolies.

American workers in the nineteenth century were subject to a double standard. They were supposed to contract freely with employers. But in fact large employers commonly did not negotiate. They offered jobs on a take-it-or-leave-it basis. If workers tried to organize and bargain as a group, they were held to be conspiring to restrain trade, while a manufacturer whose business depended on high tariffs was merely enjoying the fruits of virtue and industry. When employers conspired to fix prices, end competition, and restrain trade they were seldom punished. But when unions struck, courts frequently issued injunctions against them.

These contradictions and discrepancies undermined the doctrine of laissez-faire. Some churchgoers began to think that religion must move beyond complimenting the rich and consoling the poor. Farmers wondered why, if the government could legislate favors for business, it could not do likewise for agriculture. Younger scholars argued that classical economic prescriptions bore little relation to economic facts. Charity workers came to suspect that success or failure was not wholly a matter of character, but had something to do with environment. Big businessmen, though ostensibly the products of laissez-faire, grew increasingly unhappy with the highly competitive, and therefore uncertain, free-enterprise system. Nearly all middle-class people were upset by labor unrest. Finally, in the last third of the nineteenth century, ten million immigrants entered the country. The resulting presence of a large, often foreign-born, proletariat gave the lie to American claims to classlessness and equal opportunity, though people went on making them.

The panic of 1893 and the subsequent five-year depression showed how urgently new policies and new ways of managing affairs were needed. Americans started organizing themselves as never before. They also freed themselves to a degree from abstract concepts and self-images that had made collective action difficult earlier. Thus in the 1890s, and even more in the early 1900s, Americans at last began coping purposefully with change. Previously inhibited by doctrines that made change seem inevitable and automatic, they now came to feel that some control over the process was needed. Geographical isolation had kept men and women from knowing that others like themselves had the same wants and fears. The railroad, the telegraph, faster mails, wider reporting, more numerous periodicals brought people together, after a fashion. Better communications led to a clearer perception of common interests.

ORGANIZED LABOR

In the 1860s and 1870s most workingmen still believed in individualism and the success ethic. Through hard and intelligent work they would rise up the income scale and become profitably self-employed. Since the line between worker and boss seemed thin, early labor organizations did not make sharp distinctions between them. In 1865 the International Typographical Union allowed those "employers as may be practical printers" to join. Such a union was more a fraternal and benevolent society than a bargaining agent. Radical leaders often rejected the wage system while remaining friendly to the idea of small proprietors. The Knights of Labor—in the 1880s America's largest labor organization—saw no conflict between employers and workers, only between producers and the handful of bankers and great capitalists who were limiting opportunity. Their object was to unite all producers against the owners of unearned wealth. Samuel Gompers of the American Federation of Labor thought this naive. Gompers took it for granted that most workingmen would always be workingmen and that employers would never pay labor more than they had to. Unlike Socialists, Gompers assumed that the wage system and private property were here to stay. He had only contempt for such leaders as Terence Powderly of the Knights, who supposed that producer cooperatives would give all workingmen a stake in the profit system, thus abolishing wages and the invidious distinction between capital and labor.

Gompers managed to be both radical and conservative at the same time. He was firmly class conscious, believing that the workers must rise together. He was equally convinced that capitalism was inevitable, even desirable, so long as workers got a larger slice of the economic pie. The Knights' decline in the late 1880s brought fresh recruits to the AFL point of view. In the early 1890s the AFL beat off Socialist attempts to put it on record as favoring "the collective ownership by the people of all means of production and distribution," though barely. Tricky parliamentary maneuvers during the AFL's 1894 convention enabled Gompers to defeat a resolution to this effect, so angering radical members that he was thrown out of office for a year. All the same, federationists remained anti-Socialist, and Gompers came back to head the AFL for nearly three more decades.

Though elsewhere, notably in England, class consciousness moved organized labor toward socialism, in America it usually did not. Perhaps this was because capitalists were stronger in America, perhaps it was because bourgeois notions of advancement through the system died harder. It may also have been true that there was greater opportunity in the United States than elsewhere to climb the social ladder. In any event Gompers always had to allow for member hopes of rising to supervisory positions. Another problem was that American workers were divided by ethnic background and religion into many groups, which often hated one another. "Business unionism"—the term for Gompers's narrow approach to improving wages, hours, and working conditions for skilled workers—was uninspired compared with the grander visions of radicals. Its dominance meant there would be no great organized movement to uplift the toiling masses as a whole. Yet under the circumstances business unionism was probably all that workers could expect. Gompers's unwillingness to organize working women; narrow perspective; racism (the AFL opposed oriental immigrants, and organized blacks, if at all, in segregated locals); and complacency were typical of the skilled, mostly native-born workers he represented. Breaking with the success ethic, which was no small feat, exhausted union labor intellectually. But it did at least prepare trade unions for the age of organization just beginning.

FARMERS

Farmers, like workers, were torn between contradictory self-images. Workingmen had trouble deciding whether they were upwardly mobile or permanently downtrodden. Farmers could not decide if they were sturdy yeomen or entrepreneurs. Tradition had it that farmers were naturally virtuous and freedom-loving pillars of democracy, unlike the decadent aristocrats, wretched aliens, and greedy businessmen of urban America. But American farmers were not peasants, rooted to the earth, nor even minutemen plowing their fields with muskets at the ready. In reality American farmers had long been businessmen, growers of cash crops, attached to land values rather than to the land itself. Having illusions about themselves made it difficult for farmers to organize, as did the distances between them at a time when transportation and communication were still far from easy. Yet farm leaders made repeated efforts to overcome these obstacles, especially in the 1890s.

According to Douglass C. North, farmer discontent in the 1890s was produced by the following causes: farmers had to sell their crops at prices set by the world market, which responded to distant pressures American farmers could not always understand; foreign grain supplies rose and fell according to different rhythms resulting in unstable prices; a vast expansion of farm acreage in the United States and elsewhere led to an oversupply of commodities and depressed prices over a long period; currency did not increase as rapidly as output so that more products were competing for the same amount of money, driving prices down; and farmers, once a majority of the whole population, were becoming a minority, creating further insecurities.

Such is the view of modern economic historians. In the 1890s farmers did not see things in this way. As they understood it, price imbalances were a consequence of various "monopolies" in the economy that held the price of goods a farmer had to buy constant, while the price he got for his products was falling; railroads, grain

elevator operators, and middlemen were using monopolistic practices to absorb agricultural profits; the usurious rates of moneylend-
ers were further defrauding farmers. Much of this was true.
Mortgage interest rates were in fact somewhat higher in the West
than the East, but even this is explained by the greater risks of
farming or the greater physical distance between western farmers
and eastern sources of capital. However, farmers exaggerated the
effect of hostile business interests and minimized the influence of
impersonal economic conditions. They came to see political action as
their only hope. Earlier, farmers had organized in the Greenback
party, and in Granges and Agricultural Wheels that brought them
together for mutual help. In the 1890s they took what was apparently the next logical step and formed a mass movement, the
People's party, to redress their grievances.

The Populist party, as it was often called, had a sweeping program
that included nationalizing the railroads and telegraph lines, re-
monetizing silver at a ratio to gold of 16-1 to ease the currency
shortage, and establishing a system of federal granaries where
farmers could deposit crops in return for notes that would serve as
money. This "sub-treasury" plan would have expanded the currency while allowing farmers to store their crops until prices rose.
These excellent ideas, several of which were adopted in the 1930s,
aroused widespread, frequently hysterical, opposition. They flew in
the face of conventional economic theories and convinced otherwise
sane people that the economy would collapse if populism spread.
Conservatives attached such weight to the gold standard that talk of
going off it seemed to them not so much unwise as immoral. Colorful Populist leaders like "Sockless" Jerry Simpson, "Bloody Bridles"
Waite, and Mary E. Lease, the "Kansas Pythoness," inspired farmers
but terrified middle-class people, who saw them as the Marats and
Dantons of a new American revolution. In 1896, when Populists and
Democrats merged their tickets, President Cleveland called them
"madmen" and "criminals." Theodore Roosevelt solemnly announced that he was ready to lead a regiment into battle against the
subversive hordes rallying behind William Jennings Bryan and Tom
Watson. After the Populists were defeated the *New York Tribune*
remarked confusedly that it was "Good riddance . . . to the foul
menace of repudiation and Anarchy against the honor and life of
the Republic."

Though the campaign of 1896 was one of the most exciting presidential elections in American history, less was at stake than people at the time believed. Republicans feared that hordes of dangerous radicals were lined up behind Bryan. If he was elected, the GOP implied, these radicals would burn and pillage and prance about like devils. To avert the terrible dangers of Bryanism the Republicans raised sixteen times as much money as the Democrats. Partly this was from fear, partly because Marcus Alonzo Hanna of Ohio, chairman of the Republican national committee, was so good at his job. Hanna, known as "Dollar Mark" to his enemies, was a capitalist who more than any single person was responsible for making William McKinley president, having backed him twice for the governorship of Ohio and then organized the campaign which resulted in McKinley's nomination. Hanna, who entered the U.S. Senate in 1897, was unusually farsighted among big businessmen of his time. Though an ardent friend of private property, he also supported labor's right to organize, belonged to the moderately liberal (at that time) National Civic Federation, and understood that in the long run the best defense against radicalism was a system of capitalist economics beneficial to the average American. Even so, he was carried away by the mass hysteria of 1896 to the point of saying to a Kansas Populist, "you know you can hire half of the people of the United States to shoot down the other half if necessary, and we've got the money to hire them." These exaggerated fears united middle-class Americans against Bryan. He was further weakened by the inability of the Populist-Democrat coalition to attract enough working-class support.

Working-class people were doubtful about Populism because it promised to be inflationary, and wages tended to lag behind prices when money was cheap. Also, the Populists called for the union of all producers just when many labor leaders were rejecting the idea. Even if Bryan had won it would not have made much difference to Populists because the price of fusion had been the abandonment of nearly everything populism stood for except free silver. This was especially true in the South, where Populists had tried to organize a coalition of poor blacks and whites against the ruling white supremacist Democrats. Fusion in the South meant an end to all hope of reform there. The failure of southern Populism also intensified race hatred. Democrats had both race-baited Populists and manipulated the black vote against them in some places. Some Populists concluded after this experience that the race issue had to be taken out of politics by segregating blacks so thoroughly that the issue would never arise again. These Populists joined with racist Democrats to disenfranchise blacks and pass stricter segregation laws, a policy that was both vicious and pointless, as racism continued to poison southern politics no matter how many Jim Crow laws were passed.

Elsewhere the defeat of Populism was less harmful to farmers. New gold discoveries enlarged the money supply. The best land having now been taken up, farm commodity production did not increase so rapidly as before. In 1890 5.7 million farms were feeding 22 million urban people. In 1920 there were only 700,000 more farms, but there were 32 million additional urbanites to increase demand for farm products. Many reforms Populists had wanted —such as the income tax, the direct election of senators, postal savings banks, a more flexible currency—were achieved during the Progressive era. More important still, farmers gave up the notion that they were the "people" and concentrated on becoming an interest group. They were aided by malapportionment in Congress and in state legislatures that gave rural people more representatives than their numbers entitled them to. Although it was not until the New Deal that farmers would receive lavish federal aid, their new strategy brought some results even earlier. By 1920 the budget of the Department of Agriculture was thirty times what it had been in 1890. The Federal Farm Loan Act and the Warehouse Act, both of 1916, gave farmers the type of government assistance Populists had worked for. The Smith-Lever Act of 1914 and the Smith-Hughes Act of 1917 subsidized agricultural education. These acts foreshadowed the greater changes that were to come. Farmers, having become proportionately far less numerous than before, were now absolutely more powerful. The sturdy yeoman was gone. Farming was becoming ever more businesslike. Poor farmers moved off the land, rich ones became richer. Agriculture did not evolve as Thomas Jefferson or even William Jennings Bryan had expected. The moral and social benefits that free yeomen were supposed to confer on the Republic were now forgotten, except on ritual occasions when dead rural virtues were exhumed and eulogized.

THE MIDDLE CLASS

Industrialization, as well as a growing and increasingly more complex economy, generated a new middle class of engineers, skilled technicians, salaried bureaucrats, salesmen, and the like. These people were often well paid but also insecure. Frequently their status was poorly defined. As class alignments were shifting, it was often difficult to know who you were. Access to many professions was easy, making professional standing of uncertain value in many cases. The slogans of economic individualism, based on entrepreneurial models while the percentage of middle-class people who were entrepreneurs was shrinking, seemed less and less relevant. Business downturns and failures, which were numerous, injured the new middle class as well as the old one made up of doctors, lawyers, and business proprietors. Status fears, economic uncertainties, the novel environment created by the national market economy and the great corporations dominating it, immigration, labor unrest, farmer radicalism, corruption and inactivity on all levels of government—all combined in the 1890s to create uneasy feelings among the middle classes.

They responded to these problems in many different ways. Their most shapeless anxieties were expressed punitively. Since immigrants unsettled things they tried vainly to restrict immigration. That failing, they insisted that schools teach patriotism and indoctrinate children more effectively in American values. Groups like the Daughters of the American Revolution sprang up. Flag worship and compulsory reverence for the state were not new, but seemed all the more important at a time when it was feared that the national character was being diluted by alien beliefs. Many communities built armories and enlarged their police forces to control anarchism and other radical movements. Prohibition was advanced to encourage sobriety among immigrants especially. Like other middle-class reform movements prohibition had a rational element. But these reform movements all had elements of fantasy too. Americans differed as to what would cure the national malaise. That one did exist was widely believed, the proof of it being Populism, Anarchism, and great strikes as at Homestead, Pa., in 1892 and Pullman, Ill., two years later. Fear and frustration promoted a search for scape-goats, and for panaceas. Anarchists, immigrants, bankers, mo-nopolists, Populists were all blamed, though by different people, for what ailed America.

On another level the middle classes, old and new alike, but espe-cially the new, reacted more sensibly. If not exactly class conscious, they were certainly interest conscious. Professionals began forming associations to raise admission requirements and standardize prac-tices. Small and even some larger businessmen joined together in trade associations to influence politicians and regularize ways of doing business. Most of these organizations were aimed at practical needs and were based on the notion that in unity there is strength, an old idea which had been neglected during the preceding age of individualism. But the psychological role of these organizations was equally important. All the major elements of American society had been unsettled by change. Isolated communities, individual farmers were being tied into national networks of trade and communication. They must now respond to distant events they hardly understood, much less controlled. Organization gave them some power over their destiny, and the feeling of power perhaps even more. The same was true of city people, who without organization, and there-fore influence, were mere droplets in great, whirling, urban maelstroms. They had needs cities and traditional political machines were not able to meet, fears the old patterns of behavior could not ease. Through organization they could deal with both. Organization was the pivot around which politics and social reform would turn in the Progressive era.

A third response made by middle-class people to the problems of the 1890s involved their role as consumers. Sometimes, like farmers and workers, middle-class people defined their interests in terms of the relationships they had to the means of production and distribu-tion. At other times, because middle-class people consumed prod-ucts and services, they reacted against producers. Many consumers came to view public utilities and other interests as menaces to society, especially when they were aligned with corrupt politicians. In Wis-consin, as David P. Thelen has shown, the depression of the 1890s led people to become active in reform movements because they felt themselves victimized by these alliances. Such feelings provided a broad base for political action because, while producer orientations

divided people, consumerism united them. As workers, professionals, farmers, and the like they had different and sometimes opposite
aims. As users of electricity, water, rail service, and other things they
had much in common.

Wisconsin progressivism was based on a coalition made up of
independent businessmen, professionals, women reformers, farmers, and workers—all of whom were outraged by the same practices. When the depression hit Wisconsin certain businesses
—railroads and utilities especially—suffered revenue losses. Their
response was to raise rates. This meant that the consumer had to pay
more for these services at a time when he had less to spend. Corporations often were persistent tax evaders, thus increasing the burden
on property owners. When consumers fought against these practices they found themselves blocked by political corruption. Discov-
ering how politicians and certain business interests worked together
against the general welfare had a radicalizing effect on people. It led
them to advocate more direct democracy—the initiative, referendum, and recall, for example—in order to mobilize the power of the
people against corrupt minorities. They also came to favor regulatory laws, municipal ownership of utilities, and fairer tax policies,
among other reforms. Middle-class people found themselves
aligned with working men and women in these campaigns. Since
they needed labor votes they had to become sensitive to what labor
wanted, which, in addition to the reforms just mentioned, also
included effective factory laws, unemployment insurance, and other
benefits.

• Though the crisis of the 1890s did not immediately lead to
changes on the national level, in Wisconsin and elsewhere it produced a new kind of local politics. Before the 1890s reform meant
little more than low taxes and honest government. The terrible
depression which followed the panic of 1893 exposed the shallow-
ness of this approach. Low taxes meant that state and municipal
authorities had no resources with which to meet hard times.
Laissez-faire kept them from meeting the challenges posed by business growth and technological change. What was wanted, reformers
increasingly came to feel, was not low taxes but fair taxes. Wisconsin
became the first state to impose an effective income tax, beginning a
process that would lead to a national income tax in the Progressive
era. Liberals went on believing in honest government, but decided

that to ensure it the people must have ready access to government, hence the campaigns for direct democracy. And if the problems of an industrial society were to be met, they concluded, government would have to be more active. In the Progressive era the movement for consumer-oriented reforms would grow beyond its origins in Wisconsin, California, and other states to become a powerful nationwide force. Thus, while in one sense the 1890s was a time of frustration, it was a time of promise also. On the one hand, millions were suffering and in despair. On the other, important lessons were being learned that would bear fruit in years to come.

A final effect of the crisis of the 1890s, and the hardest to measure, was the stimulus it gave to altruism. Generations of historians have attributed the reforms and philanthropies of this period to "idealism," a vague and elastic concept that has been applied so broadly as to lose whatever value it might once have had. Yet it remains true that some changes were promoted for selfless reasons. The settlement house movement, which in America began in 1889, grew greatly during the 1890s. Though, as Jane Addams herself confessed, it gave psychological rewards to settlement workers, and thus might be considered mildly self-serving, the movement itself was firmly based on humanitarian sentiments. So was the movement toward socialism on the part of middle-class people like Victor Berger, Morris Hillquit, and Eugene Debs, who had little to gain personally from their convictions.

In a more modest way women's clubs served the same high purposes. When founded in 1890 the General Federation of Women's Clubs had only a few thousand members. By 1900 at least 150,000 women belonged. Soon memberships would rise above a million. Women of some leisure—barred by custom, perhaps also by inclination, from having careers—needed outlets for their surplus time and unused talents. Clubs were diverting, odd as that might seem considering their programs, which ran heavily to papers by members on subjects they knew little about and, what was perhaps worse, amateur recitals—practices of which the best club leaders were highly critical. Yet before the 1890s were over many clubs acquired broader interests. Locally clubwomen were supporting projects relating to community health and welfare. Nationally the General Federation began to lobby for conservation, pure food and drugs, the abolition of child labor, and other worthwhile causes.

Pity, compassion, the thirst for justice—all were heightened by the crisis of this decade, and, after 1900 especially, operated to the benefit of many kinds of disadvantaged people. Although these feelings were never as powerful as the self-interest of producers and consumers, upon which most Progressive reforms were based, they were real elements in the Progressive era all the same. Because they were so overstressed at the time, and often in later historical writings as well, some scholars have reacted by rejecting them entirely. Such discounting is useful to the degree that it corrects earlier distortions, but it runs the risk of making all public acts appear to have been selfishly motivated, which was not the case.

FOREIGN POLICY AND THE CRISIS

The principal foreign activity of the United States during the 1890s was its war with Spain. On the face of it this war did not make a great deal of sense. The United States had plenty of problems at home, and logic suggests that it would have been better off to concentrate on these rather than to engage in a foreign war. Spain was no threat to American security. Moreover, by fighting it America, then the world's leading anticolonial power, acquired colonial territories. These contradictions are more apparent than real. The Spanish-American War, though not inevitable, was an outcome of well-established national policies. The most important of these was the general agreement that expanding foreign trade was essential to the nation's economic well-being. While the late nineteenth century was in general a time of growth, progress was uneven and business downturns were frequent. There was, for example, a serious depression during the period 1873–78, a lesser one in 1882–85, and then the terrible one of 1893–97. These depressions hurt large parts of the economy, provoked labor unrest, and convinced many Americans that internal stability and dependable economic growth required an expansion of exports. This was felt most keenly by manufacturing and agricultural interests, particularly in the West. It also led the makers of foreign policy to devise long-term programs that would enhance America's position as a trading nation without at the same time burdening it with numerous colonies, as was the case with Britain, France, and other great powers.

Even before the 1890s the United States had begun strengthening its international position. The Garfield-Arthur administration was represented at an international conference in 1884 that settled the fate of the Congo. This was the first time since 1814, that the United States had participated in such deliberations with the great European powers, and it was the first time ever that Americans had joined in formal talks on colonial issues. In the closing decades of the nineteenth century the United States also negotiated many trade agreements with Latin-American countries and with Hawaii. Moreover, it began expanding the navy, which had decayed badly after the Civil War. Between 1883 and 1890 a series of naval ship-building bills were passed by Congress on the ground that they were needed to protect American trade. "While we built railroads," declared Benjamin Tracy, secretary of the navy from 1889 to 1893, "other nations built navies." By the time Tracy left office the United States had moved from seventeenth to seventh place among naval powers and was still rising. "The sea will be the future seat of empire," said Tracy, "and we shall rule it. . . . " James G. Blaine, who was secretary of state twice during the 1880s and early 1890s, had a large vision of American growth through expanding foreign trade. He felt trade agreements with Latin America and Europe would benefit the eastern United States. An enlarged trade in the Orient would benefit the American West, reducing sectional antagonisms and binding the nation more firmly together, as would an Isthmian canal. Blaine negotiated reciprocity treaties with Latin America that were expected to increase U.S. trade by lowering tariffs at both ends, and at the same time pursued a vigorous policy in the Far East. In the 1880s Korea was opened up to American commerce. When Germany and Great Britain began staking out claims to Samoa the United States entered the competition and finally became party to a three-nation protectorate over the islands.

President Cleveland took a less consistent line in foreign policy than Republican leaders in this period. For example, he was opposed to the annexation of Hawaii, which they favored. But he too considered America's commercial position overseas to be of primary importance and was ready to use force in defense of it. He employed naval power to avert a revolution in Brazil, and went to the brink of war in 1895 and 1896 to prevent Great Britain from expanding in Latin America. London held that the boundary of British Guiana included the mouth of the Orinoco River, territory that Venezuela also claimed. While blocking this expansionist move Cleveland told Congress on December 17, 1895, that it was the duty of the United States "to resist by every means in its power, as a wilful aggression upon its rights and interests, the appropriation by Great Britain of any lands or the exercise of governmental jurisdiction over any territory which after investigation we have determined of right belongs to Venezuela." This was done not out of sympathy for Venezuela, which was excluded from the proceedings that eventually vindicated her territorial claims, but to prevent the Caribbean from becoming, as Senator Henry Cabot Lodge put it, a "British lake."

When McKinley came to power in 1897 he continued the Republican emphasis on trade expansion and moved to annex Hawaii. He also resolved the crisis caused by a rebellion in Cuba that Spain seemed unable to suppress. This insurrection hurt the island and American investments there, and the longer it went on the greater the pressure on the United States to intervene. Cleveland resisted the pressure but McKinley, though it appears he hoped to avoid war, felt obliged to take action. This was necessary not just to protect American interests in Cuba, but because large sections of the American population had come to identify with the cause of Cuban independence. The Populist party platform of 1896 had endorsed Cuban independence, as had the American Federation of Labor. Mark Hanna was surprised by the insistence of Protestant clergymen that Cuba be freed from Spanish tyranny. The business community was less enthusiastic about a war with Spain, fearing that it would hurt the recovery which was just beginning.

Eventually even businessmen came to favor the war, many feeling that prolonged indecision would retard economic recovery more than the war itself. McKinley expressed this position when he noted that the Cuban issue provided "a continuous irritation within our borders" that "tended to delay the condition of prosperity to which this country is entitled." The sinking of the armored cruiser *Maine* on February 15, 1898, only gave America an excuse for what had already been decided on. Jingoes, businessmen, farmers, anti-imperialists, and imperialists alike could find common ground on this point.

The real problem for McKinley was not making war on Spain but rather making peace afterward. The war itself went easily as expected. The decrepit Spanish fleets were sunk with almost no American casualties. Even though the United States had no army to speak of, volunteers and National Guardsmen had little trouble defeating the more numerous but demoralized Spanish troops in Cuba. However, Spain's surrender revealed the deep division in public opinion over the future of Spanish colonies—except Cuba which Congress had pledged in advance not to seize. Anti-imperialists were against keeping the Philippines (Guam and Puerto Rico too for that matter) because doing so not only violated America's anticolonial tradition but was also immoral, uneconomic, and would harm democracy at home.

The imperialist argument of McKinley, Senator Hanna, and others was that annexation of the Philippines would enhance America's trading position in the Far East. The McKinley group might have been content to retain only a commercial and naval base similar to Hong Kong, but the 1899 insurrection in the Philippines made that impossible, they thought. To have a secure base the United States must take all the islands. This big mouthful was worth swallowing, expansionists felt, because the Philippines would serve to stimulate the China trade—at that time a very small part of America's overseas business, but one that generations of American capitalists had longed to expand. Popular justifications for annexation of the Philippines were often romantic, not to say hyperbolic. For a brief period some Americans were caught up in the lust for empire that possessed Britain, France, Germany, and other great powers. It was said that God wanted the United States to lead the world, perhaps in cooperation with Britain. McKinley himself said that annexation was "manifest destiny." Ministers argued that annexation would promote Christianity, a view McKinley also agreed with, though in fact Roman Catholicism was the dominant religion of the islands. McKinley gave many reasons for annexing the Philippines, but the most important was that (as he told a group of missionaries) to leave them to be snapped up by America's commercial rivals, which he was sure would happen if the United States withdrew, would be bad business.

The debate over annexation was fierce, involving matters of high policy as well as high emotion. Whereas imperialists argued that annexation was a Christian duty, William Jennings Bryan spoke for anti-imperialists by observing dryly that when "the desire to steal becomes uncontrollable in an individual he is declared to be a kleptomaniac and is sent to an asylum; when the desire to grab land becomes uncontrollable in a nation we are told that 'the currents of destiny are flowing through the hearts of men.' " Imperialists spoke of the white man's burden and duty to lead the lesser races up from darkness. Anti-imperialists made much of America's resistance to colonialism. But at bottom the debate over annexation did not turn on morality so much as on different ideas of how American foreign trade should grow. Imperialists believed in the need for naval and commercial bases in the Orient while anti-imperialists did not. Bryan felt that American interests would be adequately served by making the Philippines a temporary protectorate, as Cuba had become after the Spanish-American war. While far apart in rhetoric, and sometimes in morality, the two sides both wanted the same thing. Even if annexation had failed in the Senate, as it almost did, America's foreign policy in later years would have been much the same.

Annexation did not quite go as expected, or have the desired effects. The Philippine independence movement turned out to be far stronger than supposed, and crushing it required years of warfare, the expenditure of $600 million (more than twice what the Spanish war had cost), and the loss of perhaps hundreds of thousands of Filipino lives. Of this disgraceful episode, which saw the United States employ all the dreadful methods it had condemned Spain for using in Cuba, Mark Twain said that it made designing a flag for America's new colony easy. He suggested taking the American flag, then painting the white stripes black and replacing the stars with the skull and crossbones.

Despite the horrors caused by annexation the Republicans did not lose power in 1900 as Bryan had predicted. The return of prosperity seemed more important to voters than the acquisition of remote islands. The main feeling of people about the Philippines seemed to be irritation that the Filipinos did not immediately accept the blessings of American rule. On the other hand, annexation did not lead to the degradation of American democracy as anti-imperialists had feared.

Annexation of the Philippines gave imperialists the forward base in the Far East they had wanted. In 1900, when Japanese and European forces put down the Boxer Rebellion in China, American troops were there as well, diverted from anti-insurrection duties in the Philippines. This American presence supported the famous "open door" notes, in which the McKinley administration attacked the "spheres of influence" policy in China and called for equality of commercial treatment for all trading nations there. Over the next few years trade with China did increase substantially, though it never reached the level businessmen had hoped for.

All the same, most policy makers, even Theodore Roosevelt, came to feel that annexation had been a mistake. It became clear well before World War II made the point manifest that the Philippines were indefensible because Congress would not support a garrison there large enough to repel a major attack. Certain Philippine products competed with those of American sugar, cotton, and dairy interests, which as early as 1914 were lobbying for Philippine independence. Few Americans showed themselves interested in shouldering the white man's burden, and the hope of romantic imperialists for an American, or perhaps Anglo-American, imperium over much of the world collapsed.

Yet if the Philippine experience reinforced the country's traditional anticolonial position, it did not alter the conviction of both parties that foreign trade was vital to American success or weaken their commitment to open door diplomacy. Presidents Roosevelt, Taft, and Wilson would all insist on commercial equality abroad, and Wilson would attempt to make the principle a feature of the peace treaty after World War I. America wanted no more colonies, but it was now firmly committed to intervention abroad when necessary to protect or promote its commercial interests.

As the 1890s came to an end the stage was set for what would later be known as the Progressive era. The broad outlines of America's foreign policy had been laid down, so too had the policies that organized labor would follow until the 1930s. The end of the depression eased the political climate; hysterical fears subsided; and in a few years affluence and a measure of confidence would make new political departures feasible. During the domestic crisis many middle-class people had acquired a more urgent sense about the need for change, and this urgency would lead to practical steps on every level to modernize government and make it more responsive to the claims of various groups.

BIBLIOGRAPHICAL NOTES

An excellent study of popular ideas in the late nineteenth century is Richard Hofstadter, *Social Darwinism in American Thought* (rev. ed., 1955); see also Edward C. Kirkland, *Dream and Thought in the Business Community, 1860–1900* (1956). Still useful is Norman J. Ware, *The Labor Movement in the United States, 1860–1895* (1929). An extremely helpful survey of economic history is Douglass C. North, *Growth and Welfare in the American Past* (1966). A stimulating and important recent work is Robert H. Wiebe, *The Search for Order, 1877–1920* (1967). David P. Thelen, *The New Citizenship: Origins of Progressivism in Wisconsin, 1885–1900* (1972), is a spirited defense of progressivism as a reform movement. Thelen attacks Wiebe and others who see progressivism as an effort by middle- and upper-class interests to solve their own problems, sometimes at the expense of others, and views Wisconsin reformers much as they did themselves. The classic work on expansion is Albert K. Weinberg, *Manifest Destiny* (1935). Alfred T. Mahan, *The Influence of Sea Power Upon History, 1660–1783* (1890), is the best known of his many works. Walter LaFeber, *The New Empire: An Interpretation of American Expansion, 1860–.898* (1963), is a valuable work. William A. Williams, *The Contours of American History* (1961), is provocative. Finley Peter Dunne's pieces on current events are remarkably shrewd and entertaining; see especially his *Mr. Dooley in Peace and War* (1898).

2

THE FIRST ROOSEVELT

When a deranged young anarchist named Leon Czolgosz shot President William McKinley on September 6, 1901, few could have guessed that an age of reform was beginning. Regular Republicans had assumed that their victories in 1896 and 1900 were votes of confidence for the status quo. They saw no reason for important changes, and even if there were, hardly anyone would have thought Theodore Roosevelt the man to make them. When Roosevelt was proposed for the vice-presidency in 1900 Mark Hanna had warned that only one life stood between that "madman" and the White House. But it was Roosevelt's boisterous temperament, not his views, that was mostly at issue. In 1896, in a typically extreme statement, TR had said that Democrats represented "the spirit of lawless mob violence." He called the reforming Governor John P. Altgeld of Illinois one who "would connive at whole-sale murder." Yet other Republicans were nearly as bad. Roosevelt was a safe man even if a little excitable. The great national interests had little to fear from him.

Early on TR had announced that he meant "to be one of the governing class." He knew that in public life to get along one must go along. TR made this clear in 1884 when he supported James G. Blaine, a man of doubtful integrity but, despite this, his party's choice for president. Gentlemen like Roosevelt were expected to support Cleveland in that election, or at least abstain. But TR was not about to compromise his political future for the sake of mugwump scruples. Blaine may have given him moral indigestion; Roosevelt swallowed him all the same.

He did his duty again in 1886 when the GOP needed a spoiler candidate to run against Henry George for mayor of New York. George was a famous reformer who was challenging Tammany Hall as an independent. Republicans had little love for Tammany, but even less for outsiders who promised radical changes. As a respectable alternative to both Tammany and George, Roosevelt was perfectly suited to split the anti-Tammany vote. He ran third, hurt, no doubt, by the fact that Tammany had shrewdly nominated a reform Democrat for once. For his pains the GOP made him a U.S. civil service commissioner; a New York police commissioner; and after McKinley's triumph in 1896, assistant secretary of the navy.

Roosevelt was a patrician in politics at a time when upperclass men rarely ran for office, an athlete before it was thought correct for gentlemen to live "the strenuous life," as he called it. Roosevelt loved to box, and hunt, and fight. He longed to distinguish himself in battle and when the chance came in 1898 TR seized it avidly. After raising his own regiment, made up of aristocrats as well as cowboys, he led it in a charge up Kettle Hill in Cuba and boasted later to his friend Cabot Lodge of how he had killed a Spaniard with his own hands. His puerile cult of war and violence was, if anything, politically useful, which tells us much about moral values at the time.

After the war TR returned in glory, which he knew better than any man how to turn into votes. Through vigorous self-promotion he made himself governor of New York. As governor Roosevelt showed again his genius for public relations. He had been a favorite of cartoonists since his days as police commissioner, when his flashing teeth and spectacles became symbols of political energy. Reporters liked his informality and good humor, and besides TR was colorful and easy to write about. More important, he showed himself to be a good administrator and a careful politician. He reorganized the state government and appointed better people to office. His appointments were nearly always political, but he at least tried to get the best possible Republican for each job. Several times he went against Tom Platt, the "easy boss" of New York Republicans—though as a rule TR did what he could to stay on Platt's right side. His chief act of defiance was to put through a bill that taxed utility franchises as real property. This was also the main statutory achievement of his administration. Roosevelt believed administration, not legislation, to be the test of executive leadership, which was a convenient belief as legislatures were even more difficult for honest governors to get along with than now. TR was responsible for few major bills either as governor or president, relying instead on commissions staffed by nonpartisan experts.

Though he tried, Roosevelt did not get along with Tom Platt well enough to be certain of renomination. To get him out of New York Platt arranged his nomination for the vice-presidency in 1900. At the top of his powers, used to command, TR would have been miserable had he been forced to serve for long as the president's shadow. He was spared that by McKinley's assassination, which gave him the power he had always wanted. At the time Roosevelt's views were mostly shallow and conventional. He was against the selfish individualism of laissez-faire, but believed that while government should intervene in economic matters it ought not to impair competition. TR wished only to make competition more equitable and humane. He believed in the inferiority of colored peoples and, to a lesser extent, in that of non-Anglo-Saxons. He believed in America's destiny as a great power. To that end he encouraged foreign trade, not for its own sake as businessmen did, but as a means of extending American influence abroad. Roosevelt was prudish and felt literature should be uplifting and practical. He was against divorce, birth control, and all forms of sexual indulgence except procreation, in which he took a deep interest. Like so many WASPs Roosevelt feared that Anglo-Saxons were being outbred by fecund immigrants. To avert "race suicide" he encouraged native Americans to have large families, a dozen or so children being none too many. Whenever his friends in their travels encountered a particularly heroic example of Anglo-Saxon propagation they immediately told Roosevelt, knowing how pleased he would be.

Priggishness, racism, imperialism, and a thirst for martial glory have few admirers today, but they were not barriers to popularity in Roosevelt's time. He became the most loved and admired politician of the age, thanks to his electric personality, gift for dramatization, and keen sense of what people were worrying about. Henry Demarest Lloyd, a radical reformer, said TR had no ear for "the new music of mankind," which was true in that he was not responsive to calls for a reconstructed America such as Socialists and radical humanitarians were making. But he was quick to grasp the concerns of ordinary people—the small businessmen, prosperous farmers, skilled workers, and other middle Americans who made up his natural constituency. He also agreed in part with the less hidebound politicians of his day, who knew that traditional ways of managing—or not managing—national affairs no longer suited the changing times. This understanding, together with his own taste for aggressive leadership, would make him the first modern president.

Though highly coveted, the presidency Roosevelt took over was not the great office it would someday be. The president was little more than another factional leader. Cleveland and McKinley had shown that presidents had nearly a free hand in foreign affairs. However, at home they did nothing much but hand out jobs and sometimes veto legislation, usually because the laws were believed to be corrupt. National government was largely concerned with receiving and spending money. As it performed few services the government's income, mainly from tariff duties, sometimes outran expenses. Awkward surpluses were avoided by looting the treasury on behalf of special interests, particularly those benefiting from public works and internal improvements. There was no such thing as a national policy, only a struggle among contending factions. Under these circumstances party leadership went to men good at partisan maneuvers. The pork barrel excepted, legislation was mainly token. When it was not, as for example the Sherman Antitrust Act of 1890, reactionary judges and timid administrators kept major acts from being effective.

Roosevelt was not one to tolerate government by inertia. He reached for power as naturally as other men of his day did for wealth. He first seized control of the GOP, which Mark Hanna had made more obedient to national leaders than before. Roosevelt took command of it from him, replacing Hanna men in key jobs if they could not be won over. TR allied himself with odious but essential bosses like Boies Penrose, Matthew Quay, and Joseph Foraker. Roosevelt thus acquired powers he was not always certain how to use, except in foreign affairs where he knew his mind best.

ROOSEVELT'S FOREIGN POLICY

TR's diplomacy was straightforward and, in his own terms, successful. The Panama affair showed how he approached foreign affairs. Most national leaders wanted a canal through Central America, preferably in Panama, though Nicaragua was also considered. Agents of the financially stricken French canal company maneuvered to have Panama chosen in hopes of selling their franchise to the United States. Roosevelt favored a route through Panama, chiefly for engineering reasons, but there was one obstacle. Panama was a province of Colombia, and Colombia did not want an American-owned canal in her territory. TR told Secretary of State John Hay in the summer of 1902 that Colombians "would change their constitution if we offered enough." But when Colombia was invited to take $10 million and a small annual rental for the canal zone, it refused to sell. After Colombia's senate voted down the treaty on August 12, 1903, TR was furious, thinking that the "Dagoes," as he liked to call them, were holding out for more money—as they were, though sovereignty over the canal zone was also a sticking point. Even Dagoes could be nationalists, something Roosevelt never quite understood.

As luck would have it, a revolution broke out in Panama late in 1903, fortune being augmented by agents of the French canal company, who helped organize and finance the rising. Three days after it began the United States recognized Panama as an independent state and made a show of force to prevent Colombia from reinforcing its tiny local garrison. Panama negotiated a fast treaty with the United States (Nov. 18, 1903), granting it sovereignty over the proposed canal zone on much the same terms offered Colombia. The French canal company received $40 million for its lease. Colombia got exactly nothing. This seemed a bit rough even at the time. Later Congress did pay Colombia compensation. But TR never regretted the incident. Years afterward he sneered at his critics and said that while the debate about it went on, the Canal did too.

Roosevelt was equally decisive elsewhere in Latin America. In 1904, when the Dominican Republic was being pressed by foreign creditors, TR had its customs taken over and administered by Americans until the debts were paid. During this affair he proclaimed what became known as the Roosevelt Corollary to the Monroe Doctrine, which held that in order to prevent European countries from interfering in Latin America, the United States was free to do so herself. In expressing this corollary Roosevelt only put words to what was already an established policy. Since the British had backed down over the Venezuelan boundary in 1897 America knew no rivals in the Caribbean and would tolerate none. TR underlined that truth by sending troops in 1906 to suppress an insurrection in Cuba, where they remained for three years. It was another selfless act, like the Spanish War, according to Roosevelt. "I am doing my best to persuade the Cubans that if only they will be good they will be happy," he remarked, "I am seeking the very minimum of interference necessary to make them good."

Where America had less power, Roosevelt had less luck. Like McKinley Roosevelt wanted an "open door" in China, and so he informally supported Japan in the Far East as a counterweight to Russia. He acquiesced in Japan's takeover of Korea and hoped she would win the Russo-Japanese War. Japan did win all the battles, but exhausted her resources doing so. Had the war dragged on she would have begun to fail. So Japan asked TR to mediate a settlement with Russia, now embarrassed by defeats and weakened by the abortive revolution of 1905, which they had helped bring on. TR agreed, skillfully promoting a settlement (September 5, 1905) that was more generous to Russia than Japan expected, perhaps because Roosevelt feared Japan was growing too powerful. TR got the Nobel Peace Prize for this, surely the most bloodthirsty person ever to be so honored. The awarding of the prize did nothing to ease Japan's feeling that she had been cheated. U.S.-Japanese relations, already strained by oriental-exclusion laws in California, never quite recovered.

In December, 1907, Roosevelt sent the battleship fleet on a tour of the world. This was supposed to impress Japan with American might, but as the Japanese welcomed the fleet joyfully it may not have. Congress was less excited. It had refused to appropriate funds for a trip round the world, but TR sent the fleet to sea anyhow, reasoning correctly that Congress would not leave it stranded in Zanzibar or wherever—a novel form of blackmail that later presidents would find increasingly useful. Afterwards he said, "I determined on the move without consulting the Cabinet, precisely as I took Panama without consulting the Cabinet. A council of war never fights, and in a crisis the duty of a leader is to lead. . . . " Roosevelt was an imperialist without apologies, but not without humor. During his second inauguration in 1905 he teased the anti-imperialist Senator Augustus O. Bacon of Georgia while Puerto Rican and other colonial detachments marched on parade. After a smart contingent of native scouts from the Philippines swung by he shouted to Bacon, "the wretched serfs disguised their feelings admirably." It was hard not to like Roosevelt even when he was wrong, which to anti-imperialists was most of the time.

RESOURCE MANAGEMENT

TR's domestic political strategy until 1912 was mostly conservative. The pressure for change increased throughout his administration, but as no consensus on what sort of changes were needed emerged it was not easy to be decisive. Roosevelt ran for his first full term in 1904 promising to give America a "Square Deal," a slogan that stood for practically nothing. TR was easily reelected all the same. He was well liked. Equally important, his opponent was a Democrat so utterly obscure, even at the time, that historians remember his name only with difficulty. But a vote of confidence is not the same thing as a mandate. Roosevelt knew the people approved of him. He did not know what exactly they wanted. And though he was beginning to have ideas of his own, Congress, then a much more powerful body in relation to the executive than now, was led by old guard Republicans who did not share his views. Having but a small stick he was obliged to walk softly at times, out of caution or uncertainty or both.

On certain points Roosevelt's intentions seem clear enough. He believed in efficient government, and though he made many political appointments he also upgraded the caliber of officeholders and added 50,000 jobs to the civil service list. He used patronage for higher as well as lower purposes, making the impoverished poet Edwin Arlington Robinson a special agent of the Treasury, with the understanding that Robinson would only show up for work when the spirit moved him, which it seldom did. This was, however, not the way Roosevelt customarily filled jobs. More than any president before him TR believed in efficiency and expertise. He preferred the trained nonpartisan to any other kind of officeholder and made abundant use of special commissions. He was fully in sympathy with the movement toward rational, scientific policy making that animated progressive business leaders and applied their ideas to government wherever possible.

The change here was not so great as it seemed. The government had always used experts, and as its affairs became more complex it used more of them. Yet the old Jacksonian principle that nearly all government jobs were suitable for the average man persisted. Roosevelt believed otherwise, and though personally the best kind of generalist, surrounded himself with professionals. This was sensible inasmuch as new techniques demanded new technicians. Yet wishful thinking was involved too. Nineteenth-century individualism had promoted conflict. People like Roosevelt believed conflict was the result of ignorance, if not sometimes of selfishness as well. They believed that conflict could be greatly reduced if only the facts were made clear and rational plans devised on the strength of them. As a guide to policy making this view was not much more useful than laissez-faire, which held that only through conflict could right answers be arrived at. Competition worsened the problems it did not solve. But expertise frequently raised problems to such a level of complexity that they appeared insoluble.

Resource management was a case in point. Government had great authority over natural resources, not only by law, but also because so much of the country was publicly owned. When Roosevelt took office conservation was an established concept, and a body of experts committed to it was already in being. Legend has it that the conservation movement was a struggle between the people and the interests. As Samuel P. Hays has shown, the real issues were more complex. Most conservation leaders were not, as today, preservationists. They were typically scientists or technicians who wanted to see natural resources efficiently developed. Conservation leaders for the most part came from the applied sciences, such as hydrology, forestry, and geology. Their loyalty was to professional standards, not grass roots sentiment—whatever that might be.

Conservation grew initially out of experience gained in western water development. Irrigators believed in forests because they protected watersheds by preventing soil erosion and absorbing rainfall; they also feared that watersheds would be damaged by overcutting and overgrazing. The first national forests were set aside primarily to protect watersheds, not to conserve timber. From another point of view the new scientific school of forest managers—personified by Gifford Pinchot, who became head of the Forestry Service in 1900—believed that forests should be managed so that timber production was balanced against other uses. Hence, engineers and scientists in the new water and forest services of the federal government shared a community of interest with each other, and with some large lumber companies and irrigation groups.

Pinchot and other foresters, wanting scientific management of timber resources, were inevitably drawn to the big lumbering concerns that were able—and to a growing extent, willing—to employ more sophisticated techniques. Small operators could not afford to set aside huge tracts for discrete cutting or to make large plantings. Their way was to slash and grab and then move on. The alliance of professional foresters and timber barons Pinchot helped create gave the Forestry Service protection against Congress. The Forestry Service provided scientific assistance, performed research, fought fires, and aided the lumbermen in countless ways. They in turn used their political influence on behalf of the Forestry Service. Even so, not enough timberland was controlled by big operators or used as Pinchot thought best. In 1905 Congress was persuaded to transfer administration of the national forest to his bureau, a significant step because during TR's administration the national forests tripled in size. These great holdings were then available for private exploitation, but under conditions established by the Forestry Service.

Grazing was another tough conservation issue. The cattle industry had overstocked the public range until in 1886–87 a combination of blizzards and overuse ruined the industry (wiping out Theodore Roosevelt among other ranchers). Thereafter cattlemen became interested in breeding better stock, growing their own fodder, and other practices that meant lower immediate profits but offered more stability and prosperity over time. To end competition for limited public land they favored a licensing system. Licensing was resisted by sheepmen and by settlers who wanted to farm the range. But the idea attracted Roosevelt and his conservation experts. This led to a political deadlock. Sheepmen and farmers blocked leasing in Congress, while the alliance of cattlemen and government experts was stalemated because cattlemen opposed irrigation, which farmers and government experts favored.

Scientific resource management was one of Roosevelt's main goals, but less of this was done than he wanted. Congress did not agree with him that experts alone should make resource decisions. It also disliked his use of commissions to study and report on resource questions without consulting Congress or securing its approval. It further opposed the efforts of divisions such as the Forestry Service to become self-financing through user fees and the like. These disputes were usually described as the attempts of corrupt, reactionary, or undemocratic legislators to keep scientific conservationists from saving the country's natural resources. Sometimes this was even the case. But decision making and rational exploitation were quite separate issues. Although it was wise to build up the national forests, it was hardly democratic since the Forestry Service discriminated against small operators. Similarly, there was nothing democratic about the experts' preference for licensing, which militated against sheepmen and farmers.

All conservation issues involved conflicts between users. No doubt resources had to be managed efficiently. The national interest in them took precedence over the interest of small users, who could not afford to operate scientifically. But, if too often in the pocket of resource users, Congress was properly suspicious of government by experts. In practice the Forestry Service allowed timber operators to overcut, even devastate national forests in many places. The line between a cordial relationship and a corrupt relationship was hard to draw when private operators and a public agency became as close as the Forestry Service and the timber industry did. These problems were poorly understood at the time, as the famous Pinchot-Ballinger affair was to demonstrate.

President Taft took a narrower view of his office than Roosevelt did. He was not interested in continuing the broad resource programs Roosevelt had begun. His Secretary of the Interior Richard A. Ballinger was against many of Roosevelt's conservation policies. When Ballinger released to private ownership land and reservoir sites previously set aside for federal development, Roosevelt men led by Gifford Pinchot, who was still chief forester, tried to stop him by going over his head to President Taft. Rich, famous, a close friend of Roosevelt, Pinchot had enjoyed great influence and was slow to admit its loss. When direct approaches to Taft failed, Pinchot organized the National Conservation Association to mobilize sentiment against government policies. Taft, long-suffering as always, let this go by. Pinchot then publicly attacked Ballinger for firing a young officer of the Interior Department who had gathered material purporting to show that Ballinger had acted improperly in assigning Alaskan coal mining rights. By challenging Ballinger's integrity Pinchot obliged Taft to dismiss his chief forester (1910). Pinchot then dashed off to Africa, where Roosevelt was shooting everything he could see (which, as his eyesight had failed, was very little).

TR thought Pinchot was wrong to defy his superiors. All the same, Roosevelt had to say a few good words for his old friend and a few more for conservation. Pinchot's supporters said Ballinger was crooked and a threat to conservation. These charges were misleading. Ballinger was neither dishonest nor against conservation as such. At issue were two different approaches to resource management. Pinchot favored maximum federal control of natural resources and maximum private participation in developing them. Ballinger took a contrary view. He was a protectionist, one of those "nature lovers" as Pinchot scornfully called them, who thought that what was unique or beautiful or precious should be withdrawn entirely from commercial use. What was not should be released for private operators to develop at their own expense. Congress investigated the charges against Ballinger. Though cleared, he resigned from office in 1911.

These points of view had clashed before and would again. Protectionists, Ballinger included, fought hard but vainly to save a great valley in Yosemite National Park from being flooded to provide San Francisco with drinking water. Instead, Pinchot and Roosevelt prevailed there, as they had also in keeping national forests open to commercial use. While their policy of allocating federal funds to supply private parties with water and power lost ground during Taft's administration, it would revive later. Public money would be used to make privately held land suitable for agriculture, thus promoting farm surpluses which in later years had to be taken care of at government expense. One kind of subsidy thereby required a second, a form of double jeopardy for taxpayers that few anticipated at the time.

The Ballinger-Pinchot affair was a red herring that only further confused matters. Roosevelt supporters used it as a stick to beat Taft with, claiming falsely to be the only real conservationists. What the incident showed was that a nonpartisan government by experts such as Roosevelt envisioned was impossible. There were conflicts of interest that could not be dissolved through fact-finding and education. Where resource use was concerned, what helped one group hurt another. Roosevelt thought to bureaucratize decision making so as to make it impartial. This could seldom be done except where narrowly technical matters were concerned. Great issues did not usually involve disputed facts so much as disputing interests. To settle them required public, that is to say, political decisions. Characteristically, progressive managers—even when highly politicized, like Roosevelt—tried to remove from politics issues that were fundamentally political. They supposed that in so doing government was being made cleaner. Evil lobbies could no longer suborn congressmen if resource decisions were not Congress's to make. But what happened was that private interests merely turned their attention to government bureaus. Preservationists worked with the National Park Service. Stockmen and timber barons cultivated sweet relations with the Forestry Service. Water users rallied around the Bureau of Reclamation. Bureaucratizing decision making did not make it less partisan, only less public. Doing so created the illusion that problems were being scientifically disposed of even though favors were sought and granted as before. This deluded the public, perhaps even the bureaucrats, while doing little harm to powerful resource users.

CORPORATE REGULATION

President Roosevelt's foreign policy was based on principles he had formed much earlier. So, in a muddier way, was his policy on national resource management. But elsewhere Roosevelt was less certain. The two great pressures exerted on his administration were to regulate corporations and extend social justice. These pressures were a consequence of trends that began in the 1890s and were aggravated by the emergence of muckrakers and vocal reformers after 1900. Roosevelt did not have strong views on either subject. Both movements were resisted by conservatives whom TR did not wish to antagonize. For some time at least, neither involved well-defined courses of action upon which there was general agreement. Given these circumstances the best Roosevelt could do was stave off drastic proposals, mediate among contending factions where possible, promote enough change to give at least the appearance of progress, and stall for time in hopes that unlimited debate would eventually produce some kind of consensus. This was probably not a considered strategy. By his own admission TR believed in power and liked to use it. But in a democracy where there is little agreement on an issue there is frequently little power. Being a realistic as well as an agile politician TR made the best of his situation. The result was a program of dodges, feints, and maneuvers that brought Roosevelt through a time of many demands with his popularity and reputation intact.

Corporate regulation exemplified his problem. TR took office just when public anxiety over corporate power was at its greatest. The merger movement which triggered it was already ending, but few realized this. As Gabriel Kolko points out, the merger era had in fact been very brief. In 1895 only 43 firms had disappeared as a result of mergers and merger capitalization amounted to but $41 million. In 1898 303 firms vanished and merger capitalization reached $651 million. In 1899, the peak year, there were 1,208 firms lost and merger capitalization soared to $2.263 billion. Thereafter both figures dropped sharply. During 1895–1904 an average of 301 firms disappeared each year. From 1905 to 1914 only 100 firms a year vanished. In the whole period from 1895 to 1920 eight industries accounted for 77 percent of merger capitalization. The merger movement was thus a short-lived one restricted to a handful of basic industries. Most mergers were launched so that their promoters could make money off new stock issues. As a rule, preferred stock represented the new company's real value; common stock, the promoters' fees and expectations of future growth. The newly merged companies turned out to be less profitable than expected, which accounts in large measure for the movement's decline.

The reduction of new mergers did not help Roosevelt much. Combinations aroused deep fears that the field for enterprise was narrowing, which was the intent, though not the effect, of business consolidation. They may also have pushed up price levels. Middle-class America looked to government, armed as it was with the Sherman Act, for relief. Big businessmen, finding that mergers were not so profitable after all, looked to government for aid also. Mergers were supposed to reduce competition. But while the number of new manufacturing firms had increased by only 4.2 percent from 1899 to 1904, they grew by 25.2 percent in the next five years, even though monopolies were supposedly suppressing competition. In 1909 only one industry, iron and steel, had fewer than a thousand member firms. The rise of new companies led to a declining share of the market for merged firms. Often the merged companies earned lower profits than their several parts had made before combining. One study of 328 mergers found that only 49 percent earned profits that compared favorably with other companies in the same field. A full 40 percent of the merged companies failed. And as a rule the larger the merger the worse the performance. U.S. Steel, which commanded 61.6 percent of the market when formed in 1901, possessed only 39.9 percent in 1920. The same was true of Standard Oil, International Harvester, and others. Since mergers did not effectively restrict competition, the obvious alternative was federal regulation which would impose uniformity and, it was hoped, would stabilize conditions in each industry where the giants were flagging.

Roosevelt was faced with a great range of opinions on the trusts. Socialists and some Populists wanted government to nationalize them. Another group wanted the trusts broken up on the mistaken theory that this was the only way to preserve competition. A third, and perhaps dominant, group believed with TR that there was a difference between "good" and "bad" trusts. These people held that some trusts were the products of industrial evolution, hence natural and desirable; others, like Standard Oil, which grew rich off railroad rebates, flourished because of illicit practices and should be broken up. A fourth group, made up of big businessmen and certain intellectuals such as Herbert Croly (now often called "corporate liberals"), believed that it was government's duty to stabilize and rationalize the entire economy. Finally, there were old-fashioned people, especially medium-sized businessmen, themselves usually the most effective competitors, who felt that little if any regulation was needed.

The point of view of the last group rapidly became indefensible politically. Yet conservatives were frequently right, if sometimes for the wrong reasons. Nearly every important sector of the economy was in fact competitive. Regulation was partly a maneuver by which big business hoped to use the government's power to accomplish what the trusts alone could not do. When established, the new regulatory agencies fell under the influence of big business. For the most part they have functioned ever since as extensions of the most powerful firms in each of the industries they are supposed to monitor. There was some irony in this, but perhaps some calculation as well. Although Roosevelt seems not to have anticipated that regulatory agencies would lose their independence—to the end believing that government experts could remain nonpartisan and independent—it appears likely that the enthusiasm of some big businessmen for regulation derived from their expectation that they could use it for their own purposes.

As a consensus on regulation was not reached during TR's presidency he was forced to play the schools of thought on regulation against one another. He dismissed the Socialist-Populist idea of nationalizing the trusts on the grounds that it was immoral and un-American. Wholesale trust-busting was impractical and unwise. Both alternatives were useful, however, to the degree that they intimidated business. TR never hesitated to warn backward capitalists of the perils awaiting should reason fail to move them. He felt the argument for laissez-faire was irrelevant because there was going to be government action taken, and the only question was what it would be. But while TR believed there were bad trusts, he did not think there were many. He was also responsive to the argument that combination was inevitable, probably even desirable. Within very broad limits he was willing to promote it. On the other hand the ebb and flow of public opinion, and perhaps his own doubts, kept him from doing so consistently.

Roosevelt's reputation as a trustbuster derived largely from the indictment of the Northern Securities Company in 1902. This case was the result of a long and costly struggle between two railroad magnates, Edward H. Harriman and James J. Hill. Harriman was noted for having revived the much plundered Union Pacific. Hill controlled the Great Northern and the Northern Pacific. Harriman was backed by Kuhn, Loeb and Company and the Rockefeller group's National City Bank of New York; Hill, by the House of Morgan. Accordingly, their fight was no ordinary business conflict but a match between the two greatest aggregates of finance capital in the United States. It was waged over the Chicago, Burlington and Quincy, a small road, but one with access to Chicago, something neither the Union Pacific nor the two northern roads had. Both sides wanted the CB & Q, but it was Hill who made the highest offer, through his Northern Pacific. Harriman resolved to get the road by secretly buying control of its new parent company. Hill discovered the plan in time and both sides bought NP stock heavily, paying progressively steeper prices for outstanding shares.

As always in such cases market traders began selling short—that is, selling NP stock they did not own on the theory that soon the rivals would stop buying and the price would fall below what it was at the time they offered to sell, enabling the short trader to make a profit by delivering at a high price stock actually bought later at a lower one. But when NP stock kept rising because Harriman and Hill were keeping what they bought, short traders had to sell their other stocks in order to support their gambles. This drove the price of other stocks down without helping the position of short traders except briefly. The result was a market crash that wiped out thousands of stockholders and brokers. Kuhn, Loeb ended the crisis by suspending its demand for deliveries for a time. Short traders were allowed to settle at $150 a share, though NP stock went as high as $1,000 at one time. This reasonable compromise did not mollify an outraged public.

Even worse was to follow, as the public saw it, when the two great combinations made peace by forming the Northern Securities Company. It acquired all the shares of the Northern Pacific and the Great Northern, issuing its own shares in their place. Harriman got enough seats on the board of directors to safeguard his interests. Hill and Morgan gained a holding company so big that it could not be stolen from them as the NP nearly was. This made everyone happy except the public, which was furious. On February 19, 1902, the government suddenly announced that it was indicting Northern Securities under the Sherman Act, the first time a major corporation had been so honored.

An enraged J. P. Morgan went immediately to Washington, where he told Roosevelt to "send your man to my man and they can fix it up." But the affair was too big to fix up, and the government eventually won its case (in a Supreme Court decision of March 14, 1904). As a practical matter this ruling was of little consequence since the Morgan and Rockefeller interests were determined to have no more costly wars. Jim Hill said after Northern Securities was dissolved, "two certificates of stock are issued instead of one; they are printed in different colors, and that is the main difference." Harriman, Morgan, and H. H. Rogers of the Rockefeller group were to be among the biggest contributors to TR's campaign in 1904. The case was a great public relations stroke for TR all the same, giving him an undeserved reputation for hostility to trusts that would be useful in the short run, though embarrassing later when he would declare them to be essential.

More typical of Roosevelt's approach to business was his campaign to establish the Bureau of Corporations. Ostensibly this was a move to increase government supervision of business. TR shrewdly announced when the enabling bill came under attack that John D. Rockefeller was against it, which the public took as proof of its merit. Yet in practice most large businesses got along with the bureau after its formation in 1903. Its investigations delayed legislation that business did not like. It advocated government regulation of railroad rates, something most businessmen wanted. Shippers were resentful when privileged companies obtained railroad rebates and favored anything that would put all shippers on the same footing. Even some railroads welcomed regulation because they too disliked having to set one price for general users and a lower one for a few of their largest customers.

But devices like the Bureau of Corporations could not solve Roosevelt's dilemma. He was under pressure from three different and incompatible groups on the issue of regulation. Traditional businessmen were against it. Consumers increasingly favored it for the sake of lower prices and improved services. They saw regulation as an aggressive instrument. Sophisticated businessmen wanted regulation, but only if it meant less competition and higher prices. To them, regulation was a benevolent tool of business. There was no way these competing demands could be satisfied, for measures pleasing to one constituency would inevitably offend the others. Meat inspection was a case in point. Public interest groups wanted regulation to increase competition; to reduce prices; and, after the appearance of Upton Sinclair's muckraking novel *The Jungle* (1906), to raise the quality of meat products. The large packers were friendly to benevolent regulation in theory if it did not raise the costs of doing business too much and enabled American products to be sold in those European countries from which they had been barred for health reasons. Smaller packers were generally against regulation both in principle and because any higher costs would reduce their ability to compete with the big Chicago packers. Roosevelt and the Congress were dragged into regulation by the general outcry and produced the Meat Inspection Act of 1906. This act satisfied both consumer demands for higher quality and the desire of big packers not to have their costs raised excessively (the expense of inspection was borne by the government). It was opposed by small packers, but also by the large ones as it did not reduce competition sufficiently. On balance the act probably did Roosevelt more good than harm. Even so, as it upset important business groups it still represented the kind of step he preferred to avoid.

So also did the Pure Food and Drug Act of 1906. This act too was supported by consumers, aided by Dr. Harvey Wiley, chief chemist of the Department of Agriculture. It was welcomed by some producer organizations for the reassuring effect it would have on the food and drug buying public. But it was resisted by others as an infringement on their liberties and a threat to competition. Both these acts were probably most effective in raising the quality of food and drugs, least effective when it came to lowering prices and restricting the trusts. Their tendency was to raise prices and limit competition, but not by much. Thus they antagonized the smaller and more aggressive firms without at the same time benefiting larger concerns—at least in the short run.

TR's complex relation to business was dramatically illustrated by the panic of 1907, itself a key event in the history of federal regulation. The economy turned down in 1907, leading Roosevelt to complain that businessmen were sabotaging his reforms. Certain businessmen charged that trust-busting and threats of regulation were destroying confidence and depressing the market. Many of them had never accepted the case for regulation and saw each step away from laissez-faire as a threat to business. Paranoia worsened in September, when the Union Pacific tried to float a bond issue of $75 million and only $4 million was taken up. In October several trust

companies failed after trying to corner the copper market. This led
to runs on other banks and the panic was on.

J. P. Morgan returned from a church conference to take command on the 20th of October. Big bankers and financiers met at his
great library to learn what they must do to be saved. Morgan ordered the books of all major financial houses opened to his men so as
to determine who was in trouble and what it would cost to help them.
Meanwhile, the Knickerbocker Bank failed. Its fourth vice-
president said the panic was the fault of TR, who had destroyed the
country's credit system. Roosevelt blamed it on "Pierpont Morgan
and so many of his kind." Undiscouraged, Morgan went on stem-
ming the tide. The strongest banks loaned money to the weakest.
Secretary of the Treasury George B. Cortelyou agreed to deposit
more federal funds in New York banks. On October 23, when the
Trust Company of America experienced a run, Morgan sent mes-
sengers with cash to meet depositor demands. He forced trust company presidents to form an association for mutual support. Secretary Cortelyou put another $10 million in national banks, which was
then loaned to threatened trust companies. Several small houses
failed. The run on TCA continued.

On the 24th Morgan drove through cheering crowds to Wall
Street, where he had been called to save the stock market. The
exchange president wanted to close its doors as no call money
(short-term loans) was available to finance stock transactions. Morgan raised $27 million in five minutes, driving the interest rate on
call money down from 100 to 10 percent. On the 25th he raised
another $13 million to keep the exchange open. He saved the city of
New York from bankruptcy by arranging a loan of $30 million,
enabling it to redeem short-term bonds.

When Moore and Schley, a leading brokerage house, threatened
to go under, Morgan benefited both the market and himself. The
firm's principal assets were Tennessee Coal and Iron Company
bonds, in normal times as good as gold. But with money so tight
Moore and Schley could not borrow against them. Morgan arranged
for U.S. Steel (which he had organized) to buy the bonds, nominally
as a public service, although really because TC & I holdings would
strengthen U.S. Steel enormously. Morgan told Roosevelt that nothing less would avert a crash. Roosevelt, who knew little of such
things, waffled. On the one hand, he refused to give "any binding

promise" not to prosecute USS under the Sherman Act. On the other, he told Morgan to go ahead. USS bought a controlling interest in TC & I for $45 million, which encouraged the stock market. No one cared to remind Morgan that he had promised to ruin anyone who took advantage of the crisis. Next Morgan got the strong trust companies to support the weaker with another $25 million, by locking the bankers in his library overnight until fear and exhaustion wore them down. The Bank of England then sent over $10 million in gold and the panic was broken.

The crisis had little effect on old guard financiers, who were used to panics and, in any case, would rather have died than surrender a conviction, however obsolete. It was different with progressive businessmen. Already dissatisfied with the banking system, they were now certain it had to be changed. Capitalism could not go on expecting Morgan to save it. He was old. Financiers were losing ground—casualties of economic growth, the failure of merged companies to perform well, and the increasing ability of corporations to generate through profits the money needed for further expansion. None of his heirs would have the power of a J. Pierpont Morgan. Key businessmen, knowing that the panic could not have been stopped without the $35 million deposited by the Treasury in New York banks, were ready for government intervention. So was Roosevelt, but he wanted more than bankers did. TR had earlier proven he was no enemy of bigness by allowing the House of Morgan to create International Harvester and buy TC & I for U.S. Steel. Before the panic he had already shown in the case of railroads that he expected big business to play by certain rules. Roosevelt cared little about tariff reform, but wanted railroad regulation very badly. In his second term he traded off the one for the other in a dazzling show of political skill. When the roads objected he said regulation was the only alternative to nationalization. This resulted in the Hepburn Act of 1906, authorizing the Interstate Commerce Commission to set railroad rates.

After the panic of 1907 Roosevelt asked Congress for a host of changes, including federal incorporation and regulation of all interstate business, federal regulation of the stock market, curbs on labor injunctions, compulsory investigation of labor disputes, extensions of the eight-hour law for federal employees, and personal income and inheritance taxes. Neither business nor labor were ready for all this. Regulation was a medicine business would only take in small doses—and only when the advantages to it were obvious. Labor wanted freedom from the courts, but also from government. Union leaders feared compulsory investigation would lead to compulsory arbitration, which they detested as it would make them unnecessary. Roosevelt understood these qualms and did not push his ideas hard, even though he told friends that reform was the only alternative to revolution. Whether TR actually felt "predatory wealth" would bring on socialism is unclear. There is no doubt that he disapproved of both laissez-faire and public ownership of the means of production. His own alternative, which would later be called the "New Nationalism," was foreshadowed by George Perkins in a speech given just after the panic.

Perkins was called J. P. Morgan's secretary of state because he supplied that human touch which the great Pierpont lacked. He was probably the first great industrial front man. He polished a company's image when production men got it dirty. Perkins, a partner at the House of Morgan, was chairman of the all-important finance committee of U.S. Steel, where he established a profit-sharing plan no worker could afford to join. Perkins advocated the eight-hour day, but at USS the twelve-hour day and the seven-day week remained standard throughout his life. Perkins was acclaimed for his vision all the same. He was friendly with John Mitchell of the United Mineworkers and spoke warmly of labor's rights even while resisting them. To his mind these rights did not include collective bargaining. Perkins never let his enthusiasm for social justice interfere with profits, just as Roosevelt's altruism never interfered with politics. Both men shared the conviction that what was good for them was good for the country. This community of taste and interest, plus Perkins's absolute loyalty to Roosevelt, was the rock on which their friendship was built.

Early in 1908 Perkins spoke on "The Modern Corporation" at Columbia University. In this address, which pointed the direction Roosevelt would go, Perkins announced that cooperation, not competition, was the fundamental law of life. Great corporations showed this to be true. Products of advanced technology, they eliminated waste and made efficient use of men and materials. They brought savings through standardization, better marketing, and better research. Corporations steadied employment and raised wage levels.

They enabled industry leaders to cooperate intelligently with one another. Since no individual or group could own a giant corporation, as a business organization it was more democratic, less subject to nepotism and personal influence than a smaller firm. Self-interest forced great corporations to take socially responsible positions. While corporations were not quite perfect yet, mainly because state laws differed, federal regulation would make them so.

This was mostly nonsense. Big combinations were frequently less efficient than smaller firms. Having many stockholders did not make a company more democratic because ownership was then divorced from control. The social conscience of corporations was all but invisible, except when bad publicity made a show of benevolence necessary. Big companies drove wages down whenever they could, U.S. Steel being a leader in this regard. When businesses did cooperate with each other, mainly it was to lobby government and fix prices. The point, however, is not that Perkins was wrong, though he was, but that his analysis promised an end to the struggle between capital and labor. In effect he and Roosevelt were saying that if trusts were effectively regulated and labor given a fair shake, the public interest would be served. This became evident soon after his speech when Perkins had Congressman William P. Hepburn introduce a bill empowering government to approve "reasonable" agreements between corporations, providing only that they were submitted for approval to an "appropriate body." If their deals were not voided within thirty days the contracting parties were to be immune from prosecution.

The Hepburn bill would have legalized monopolies. It meant getting federal incorporation through the back door. The quid pro quo was that Hepburn's bill would also have exempted unions and strikes from prosecutions under the Sherman Act. This was essential to win labor support, and even more perhaps to show that the bill was not just an expression of corporate self-interest. Though crucial, the labor exemption could not be sold to Congress, even though endorsed by TR after a fashion. In March of 1908 he sent a special message on the trusts to Congress which said that "in the modern industrial world combinations are absolutely necessary." Of the Hepburn bill he wrote "some such measure as this bill is needed in the interest of all engaged in the industries which are essential to the country's well being." Yet when medium and small businessmen attacked the bill for giving immunity to trade unions TR let it die. Perkins did not lose hope. In 1910 he resigned from the House of Morgan to promote his ideas, which two years later he would write into the Progressive party platform.

SOCIAL JUSTICE

Roosevelt handled social justice issues much as he did the trusts. He was sympathetic to both, but was politically constrained from doing much for either. Since humanitarians had less power than big business they got less. The social justice movement wanted laws insuring pure food and drugs; abolishing child labor; strictly regulating the hours and conditions of working women and children; providing an eight-hour day; removing legal obstacles to trade unionism, workmen's compensation, a minimum wage, and related measures. Some of these were purely matters of health and welfare that Roosevelt found easy to endorse. But the heart of the social justice movement concerned labor's rights.

Like many progressives Roosevelt could not make up his mind about trade unions. On the one hand, like trusts, they appeared to be natural products of industrial growth; on the other, conspiracies in restraint of trade. Labor unions were compatible with the New Nationalism he would call for in 1910. Yet Roosevelt had to face both popular prejudice and his own negative feelings about unions. At the time it was usual to condemn both trusts and trade unions. If forced to choose between them, however, middle-class people generally preferred trusts. There were no compelling reasons for this. Corporations were immensely more powerful than unions, and a greater threat to free enterprise. Union demands, if granted, pushed up prices sometimes; so did monopolies when they could. Probably the double standard was a matter of class loyalty. People seemed to feel that while trusts were bad, they were at least bourgeois, whereas unions were both bad and different, composed of aliens and anarchists, given to strikes and mob violence.

These views, plus his own doubts, kept Roosevelt from getting very close to trade unions. All the same, he was the first president to interest himself in labor's problems. In 1902 he helped mediate a bitter strike of anthracite coal miners, rather than sending troops to break it as sometimes happened. Roosevelt supported legislation regulating the wages and hours of working women and children, extending the eight-hour day, making employers liable for accidents, and limiting the use of injunctions against strikes. Few of these bills passed. The social justice movement was poorly organized in TR's time and lacked the muscle it would possess briefly later. Still, Roosevelt seemed to have his heart in the right place and retained the good will of labor leaders and reformers without actually giving them much, a fine political art which he practiced better than anyone.

The Roosevelt presidency was both less and more than it appeared. It was less because few important laws were passed—a fact obscured by Roosevelt's great talent for public relations. He was good at substituting drama for progress. This inaction was partly a result of his conservative streak, partly the consequence of divided opinion. Where there was no agreement Roosevelt had to get by with public spectacles. If he could not lead he could at least amaze. This made him the most popular figure of his time.

TR's presidency was important in other ways though. Roosevelt was the first modern president because he understood how to use his office as, in his words, "a bully pulpit," and because he expanded the powers of that office. He was the first national president since Andrew Jackson, in that he appealed to many sections and classes, even though local conditions kept him from cracking the "solid South." Unlike Jackson, who used his popularity to weaken government, Roosevelt employed his to strengthen it. Before Roosevelt people were not in the habit of looking to Washington for help. Afterwards, they increasingly did. Thus began the tradition of the powerful central government led by a "strong" president.

Roosevelt was the first president to take a continuously active part in world affairs. Although earlier presidents had enlarged the navy and intervened abroad, none before him claimed the right to become involved where the country did not have large interests at stake, as Roosevelt did during the Russo-Japanese War and during the Algeciras conference of European great powers in 1906. He regarded national power as others did religion. Before Roosevelt it was always possible, though not always true, to say that America became involved abroad by accident or in self-defense. After Roosevelt the pretense of isolation from world affairs could not be so readily sustained. TR obliged all his successors to admit that America was a great power, and they had to bear the consequences, however unpleasant. Roosevelt has in the past been awarded high marks by diplomatic historians who seemed to think the use of force its own reward or, more often, that American force was somehow more benevolent than other kinds. Since Vietnam the readiness to use force has come to seem less admirable, as has interventionism generally. In the future Roosevelt may be admired more for his conservation policies than for his foreign policy. Even though he sometimes advocated unwise resource programs, Roosevelt enlarged the national forests from 42 to 172 million acres, established 51 wildlife reserves, and created 13 national monuments, including the Grand Canyon and valuable archaeological sites. Whatever his faults, Roosevelt did more than any single figure in American history to save the national heritage.

BIBLIOGRAPHICAL NOTES

A most entertaining study is Henry F. Pringle, *Theodore Roosevelt: A Biography* (1931). William Henry Harbaugh, *Power and Responsibility: The Life and Times of Theodore Roosevelt* (1961), is more sympathetic. An important evaluation of TR's foreign policy is Howard Beale, *Theodore Roosevelt and the Rise of America to World Power* (1956). A valuable work is Samuel P. Hays, *Conservation and the Gospel of Efficiency: The Progressive Conservation Movement, 1890–1920* (1959). Gabriel Kolko, *The Triumph of Conservatism: A Reinterpretation of American History, 1900–1916* (1963), argues persuasively that reform was a tool of business interests. Though I am much in debt to this study I feel it gives too little weight to ignorance, accident, the fact that the consequences of actions are sometimes unintended, and to the genuine altruism of many Progressives. A book which supports Kolko in many respects is Robert H. Wiebe, *Businessmen and Reform: A Study of the Progressive Movement* (1962). Also useful is John A. Garraty, *Right-Hand Man: The Life of George W. Perkins* (1960).

3

TAFT AND THE STRUGGLE FOR REFORM

William Howard Taft was one of the fattest and most unhappy presidents in American history. Had he been thin he would still have been downcast: he was after all temperamentally unsuited to the job; he followed one of the country's most vigorous and admired presidents; and he was a conservative who by accident held office during an age of reform.

Roosevelt seems to have picked Taft as his successor partly because at bottom TR was a conservative too—though infinitely more flexible and farsighted than most. His favorites, the majority of them near-reactionaries such as Elihu Root, were wildly unsuited to follow him as president. Taft had been loyal to Roosevelt, and he was discrete. He was not aligned with either the right or left wing of the party at the time, making him acceptable to both. Perhaps also Roosevelt wanted whoever succeeded him to be mediocre, thus putting his own presidency in an even better light. Taft, though a capable administrator, was not likely to outshine Roosevelt. He had every quality needed to reach the White House and almost none that would be of use once he got there. Taft did not even want to be president, having taken the nomination in 1908 mainly to please his wife. The Democrats sealed his fate by nominating their old champion William Jennings Bryan, out of nostalgia and a desperate shortage of talent. But Bryan's day was over and Taft won the election almost by default.

LOCAL REFORM

Taft believed in the status quo and agreed with regular Republicans on everything except tariff reform, which he favored. But he took office at a time when the demand for change had reached a point where it could no longer be denied. Mostly this was because progressives had gained enough strength in the cities and states to win congressional elections. These new men were not all of one mind since progressivism meant different things to different people. Local reformers were interested in having efficient, honest, and responsive government. Some local leaders, like Mayor Tom Johnson of Cleveland, were humanitarians. Many were organized around issues affecting them as consumers and taxpayers. They were against the old politics built around ethnic groups and producer organizations. They upheld the concept of a public interest against the politics of special interests. Some reformers, like Robert La Follette of Wisconsin, managed to combine humanitarianism with efficiency. Others had narrower ambitions. The wants of progressive local businessmen were best expressed by the movement for the creation of city managers and city commissions. As early as 1896 John H. Patterson of National Cash Register had said that "a city is a great business enterprise whose stockholders are the people." Business leaders were annoyed by corruption, but even more by government's inability to meet their need for increased public services. Economic expansion and technological change had put great strains on local government. It had to supply power, water, mass transportation, police, and fire protection to growing numbers of people. Yet, while taxes went up, services did not improve as much as businessmen thought they should.

Galveston became the first city to achieve efficient local government because in 1901 it was lucky enough to be hit by a tidal wave.

The city was bankrupt and unable to cope with disaster. A group of businessmen then took over and announced that they saw Galveston "not as a city but as a great ruined business." They established a five-man commission that functioned both as council and mayor. Within five years Galveston's city bonds were selling above par. The city had been physically rebuilt, while annual budgets were running at about a third less than before the tidal wave. This proved that efficient government was possible. The "Galveston plan" was not the final answer though. Eventually most cities that changed over to commission government adopted a refined version that had an appointed city manager serve as executive officer of the commission. But however modified, the commission plan was good enough to lead hundreds of cities to adopt it during the Progressive era.

Though city reformers often claimed to be democratic, they frequently were not. Thanks to the work of Samuel P. Hays, Pittsburgh offers a well-documented example of what civic betterment sometimes meant in practice. Like many American cities at the turn of the century Pittsburgh had a decentralized government. Its council was made up of representatives from each of the many Pittsburgh wards. Each ward had its own school system. A citywide political machine held the wards together, though loosely. In most respects political power was based in the neighborhoods. This was not a particularly modern or efficient system, but it was a representative one. Of some 387 council and school board members who held office before the reform, 67 percent were small businessmen, clerks, and workingmen. Elected to protect local interests, they were mainly concerned with public works, handing out jobs, and protecting their wards from outside pressure. This was precisely why reformers meant to destroy the ward system. Corporations wanted uniform policies advantageous to business. Teachers wanted a centralized school system. Physicians wanted a citywide public health program. This kind of progress was impossible so long as power remained in the hands of traditional ward leaders.

In 1910–11 these interests united to overthrow the system. About half the reformers were officers of large corporations or the wives of officers. The other half were professionals allied with the business elite. As this elite controlled only a few wards there was no question of voting reform in. Rather, the elite used its influence in the state legislature to have a new charter forced on Pittsburgh that replaced the old council with a much smaller one whose members were elected at large. Few of the old council members were known outside their wards or had enough money to campaign throughout the city, giving the elite a big edge. At the same time the many school boards were replaced by a single board, whose members were appointed by judges of the Court of Common Pleas. The result was that the new city council and school board, with but one exception, were composed of business and professional leaders. They put through changes that made for uniform, if not necessarily humane, government.

Pittsburgh was by no means unique, which is not to say that urban reform was always a matter of one set of special interests replacing another. Although reformers believed that what was good for them was good for everyone, reform officials were generally less corrupt and more conscientious than machine politicians. They were also often obliged to accept popular demands for measures like the initiative, referendum, and home rule, which were thought (wrongly, on the whole) to promote democracy. The point is that while reform was promoted in the name of democracy, and even of humanity, and was sometimes made to seem a struggle between the people and the interests, on every level of government it was frequently only a matter of rationalizing obsolete and inefficient political structures. As the new mechanisms were designed by businessmen and professionals, those groups naturally profited most from innovation. Social justice was not inconsistent with their aims, but neither was it a necessary consequence. Thus, in Pittsburgh there was reform without social justice, while in La Follette's Wisconsin the two went together. Even so, while Wisconsin was often seen as the premier example of the people rising up to crush the bosses, it differed from other progressive states only in degree.

Wisconsin progressivism was led by Robert M. La Follette, one of the most remarkable men in American political history. Aloof, unbending, incorruptible, he was a great orator through force of character rather than demagoguery. La Follette was capable of holding audiences of farmers spellbound for hours while he recited tariff schedules. Of course formal oratory was much more important in those days than it would be once the modern mass media came along. People had fewer diversions and longer attention spans. La Follette's political career was based on his having won a regional oratorical contest while studying at the University of Wisconsin. This made him a local celebrity overnight, the guest of honor at a special reception in the State House, and a man known through newspaper accounts to just about every farmer in the county. People valued long, formal addresses and read newspapers closely, habits that radio and television had not yet corrupted.

Politically conventional at first, La Follette became an insurgent after falling out with the state Republican party's leadership. He was also much influenced by local reformers who had begun working for change before his conversion. He started building his own organization, and though he failed of the Republican nomination for governor twice before gaining control of the state convention in 1900, he finally built a disciplined machine so strong that it dominated Wisconsin politics for generations. This was done without a primary system or any of the devices—such as the direct election of U.S. senators, the initiative, referendum, and recall—that progressives believed essential to good government. La Follette's success flowed instead from developments that began in the 1890s, when the depression created a desire for change. The public had grown tired of high taxes and inefficient government. Monopolistic utilities faced with declining revenues raised rates, leading to demands for regulation or municipal ownership. People were already organizing around these issues before La Follette came to be seen as the man most likely to beat the regulars.

La Follette claimed his power was a simple matter of the people knowing virtue when they saw it. But in reality, by broadening his aims, he had been able to unite two different constituencies. Poor farmers and workingmen liked his programs for social justice and welfare. Middle-class people were determined to abolish favoritism and rationalize government. Moreover, as he painstakingly showed in his autobiography, La Follette was eager to improve business conditions by adding services and modernizing state government. The political machine he destroyed was closely tied to railroad interests that enjoyed many special favors. These were resented by shippers, including farmers, as well as by other businessmen who did not enjoy the same tax breaks. La Follette and his progressive successors in Wisconsin obtained the direct primary and taxation of railroads at value, a state income tax, a corrupt practices act, an industrial commission to supervise working conditions, a minimum wage law for women, the reduction of child labor, workmen's compensation, a state commission to set railroad rates, and other reforms. Appropriations for the state university were tripled, pushing it into the front rank of American universities, where it has remained ever since.

The case of Wisconsin was admired by humanitarians for its contributions to social justice. But part of La Follette's strength was based on his having made Wisconsin a good place for business as well as a good place to live in. Corporations were encouraged to settle in Wisconsin, where they would be taxed fairly. The railroads learned after being forced to cut rates that lower fares generated more traffic. And their costs declined because they were no longer allowed to give rebates or to issue the free passes that formerly bought the sympathy of politicians and newspapermen. In 1907 other utilities were regulated, and they too discovered that lower charges meant added business. In fact statemade regulation was supported by utilities as an alternative to more drastic measures on the local level. The state forests were enlarged, which helped tourism become one of the state's largest industries. Insurance regulation, banking regulation, and similar devices led to better business practices and fewer bankruptcies. La Follette made maximum use of experts to advise government and staff important agencies. In consequence Wisconsin had as efficient a government as was possible at the time. Businessmen welcomed these new agencies, La Follette was proud to say, "simply because the regulation is scientific." Nearly everyone gained from equitable taxation and improved public services.

NATIONAL REFORM

Not all movements for change were so barren socially as in Pittsburgh, nor so fruitful as in Wisconsin. Local businessmen were generally more eager for municipal than national reform, because city government was both more accessible and more important to them. But by 1910 or so there was broad agreement in the United States that politics as a whole had to be modernized. And those who felt this way were beginning to send people to Congress. La Follette himself was one of the early arrivals, after being elected to the Senate in 1906. He was soon joined by others, some, like William Borah newly elected, others, such as Jonathan Dolliver, former regulars who knew it was time to switch. This made conflict inevitable since the GOP, which controlled Congress, was still run by conservatives who were comfortable in the nineteenth century and had no intention of leaving it, still less of sharing their power with progressive upstarts.

Taft was hardly the man to preside over so badly divided a party, as he quickly demonstrated on taking office. He personally disliked "Uncle Joe" Cannon, Speaker of the House, and he was also strongly committed to tariff reform. When Cannon made a high tariff speech Taft decided that he and the Republican insurgents, who also favored lower tariffs and wanted to reduce Cannon's power, were on the same side. Because the tariff is now seen as essentially a technical problem, it is hard for us to understand the passions surrounding protection then. It had been a central political issue for generations, at times almost the only political issue. In a broad way Democrats, led by the agrarian South, favored low duties while Republicans, especially from the industrial Northeast, favored a high protective tariff. Tariffs were not a matter of class because it was widely believed in industrial areas that high wages and high profits alike depended on protection. Accordingly, many labor leaders joined with businessmen in lobbying for it.

When in the majority, congressional Democrats had tried to lower tariffs significantly, but were frustrated by defections on the part of representatives from industrial areas. As Republicans were usually solid on the issue, a handful of Democratic votes were enough to save protection. By 1909, however, important changes had taken place. Ten Republican senators from the Midwest, led by Robert La Follette, together with a group of Republican congressmen, turned against protection because the progressive elements they represented had grown more interested in consumer problems than in the needs of producers. Prices seemed to be rising faster than incomes, and tariff reform appeared essential if standards of living were to be maintained. Many progressives believed that monopolists were growing rich at the expense of the public from tariffs that enabled them to maintain prices at unreasonably high levels. They felt reform would weaken the power of special interests at the same time as it benefited consumers. These Republican insurgents challenged the regular leadership and were not afraid to ally themselves with progressive Democrats if necessary. The insurgents viewed the old guard as tools of arrogant wealth. The GOP's conservative leadership, on the other hand, regarded insurgency as treason. This combination of self-interest and ideology made the fight for tariff reform one of the bitterest political struggles in modern history.

Since Cannon was a mainstay of the protectionist forces, Taft agreed at first with the insurgents that tariff reform and a reduction in the Speaker's power were related issues. But when Taft called a special session of Congress in 1909 to revise the tariff law he was told by Senator Nelson Aldrich and Representative Sereno Payne, chairman of the House Ways and Means Committee, that if he did not back Cannon there would be no tariff reform. So Taft threw his support to Cannon, who survived the first insurgent attack. But, led by Congressman George Norris, the insurgents regrouped; after holding Congress in session for thirty-six continuous hours, they changed the House rules to cut the Speaker's powers. Taft had sided with the regulars just in time to go down with their ship. Worse was to follow. When the new tariff law reached the Senate, Aldrich put in so many amendments that the new rates, while different, were not much lower than the old ones. The president had sold out for nothing. Taft further compounded his errors by defending the Payne-Aldrich Tariff, not as the best tariff he could get, which it probably was, but as the "best tariff ever passed by the Republican party," something no one in the Midwest where he was speaking believed for a moment.

Payne-Aldrich was Taft's Stalingrad. Whatever lingering respect the insurgents had for him was gone. The new tariffs aroused the fury of midwesterners and glued congressional insurgents together more tightly than before. Taft further alienated them by supporting Secretary of Interior Richard Ballinger against Chief Forester Gifford Pinchot, in their bitter controversy over the conservation of natural resources, a move taken to mean that he was against conservation. As if he did not have enough enemies, Taft then went on to offend big business by enforcing the Sherman Act with unusual vigor. He brough forty-four indictments against corporations, more than Roosevelt or any president before him. Standard Oil and the tobacco trust were ordered broken up as a result of actions begun in Roosevelt's administration. But when Taft brought new indictments against U.S. Steel and International Harvester TR was furious. Both were J.P. Morgan firms in which George Perkins had been active.

And the U.S. Steel indictment was based on its acquisition of Tennessee Coal and Iron, a move Roosevelt had personally approved, even though misled by Morgan on the particulars.

These strains began breaking the GOP up. In 1910 Wisconsin regulars seceded from the La Follette organization and formed their own state Republican party. Taft Republican clubs sprang up in the Midwest, wherever insurgents had gained control of the party. Democrats took control of the House that year, often at the expense of Republican regulars. This weakened the old guard, but not its devotion to obsolete policies. In 1911 La Follette's congressional insurgents formed the National Progressive Republican League, which also included six senators and eight governors. Ostensibly the league was to promote the direct election of senators and other progressive schemes. Mostly it was a vehicle for La Follette's presidential hopes. TR was asked to join but declined on the grounds that Taft's renomination could not be prevented.

La Follette believed that Roosevelt was already plotting to run again himself. Roosevelt was indeed under great pressure from his old supporters, who felt Taft had betrayed them. Also, TR was restless in private life. He had been moving toward a set of policies that would soon be called the "New Nationalism" program, something he alone could put over. La Follette later said Roosevelt had decided to run after making a successful speaking tour in 1910, but wanted someone else as a stalking-horse to see how much anti-Taft sentiment there was in the country. La Follette claimed that TR had indirectly assured the Wisconsin senator of his support. In any event a convention of progressive Republicans from thirty states met in Chicago on October 16, 1911, and passed resolutions urging La Follette to run for the nomination. He tried, but did not get far. What worked in Wisconsin did not go down as well in the country at large.

Meanwhile Roosevelt began sounding more and more like a candidate. By early 1912 many progressives were looking for some way to switch from La Follette to Roosevelt. La Follette gave them the chance in February, when he spoke to the Periodical Publishers' Association in Philadelphia. Overtired, not yet recovered from food poisoning, and worried about his daughter's illness, he made a bad scene. His supporter Congressman Henry Allen Cooper of Wisconsin wrote later that La Follette rambled and, when people walked out, shook his fist at them. He repeatedly lost his temper. La Follette's private secretary said to Cooper, "this is terrible—he is making a d——d fool of himself." Cooper finished his memo with the prophetic line, "it ends him for the presidency."

La Follette's behavior opened the way for TR who, as La Follette was no longer considered a serious candidate, could not be accused of splitting the progressive Republican vote for selfish reasons. But Roosevelt still found himself in a difficult situation. To beat Taft at the convention he needed the midwestern insurgents who had first rallied to La Follette. But the insurgents were against the trusts, whereas Roosevelt, who had never minded them much, now favored business combinations. Like most good politicians Roosevelt was never a very firm ideologist, consistency being the hobgoblin of losers. Yet with certain other progressives he had been developing a vision of American political and economic life that was very different from the Victorian prescriptions still in vogue when he became president.

THE NEW NATIONALISM

Before 1912 this new sense of how American life should be organized was best expressed by the National Civic Federation. The NCF was founded in 1900 by men who believed in government action against unfair competition and market instability. They wanted the ideology of laissez-faire replaced by a new creed involving a collective responsibility for the common good within "the industrial and commercial framework which is the indispensable shelter of us all," as one spokesman put it. The NCF was imbued with the ideas of social engineering and efficiency so popular at the time. It favored conciliation, rationalization, and, to a degree, humanitarianism. From the start its members represented not only business, but the public, and even labor. They included Mark Hanna, the NCF's first president; Samuel Insull; Charles Francis Adams; Andrew Carnegie; members of the Morgan group; Samuel Gompers, who was its first vice-president until his death in 1924; Grover Cleveland; and such famous university presidents as Nicholas Murray Butler, Charles W. Eliot, and Benjamin Ide Wheeler.

The NCF saw its chief enemies as "the Socialists among the labor people and the anarchists among the capitalists." By "anarchists" was meant those old-fashioned individualists who wanted only to smash unions and beat the competition, by fair means or foul. In practice, most resistance to the NCF came from small and medium-sized businessmen who were bitterly antiunion and intensely competitive. They were represented by the National Association of Manufacturers, a far less sophisticated body than the NCF. The NCF's sympathy for labor was less than wholehearted, however. Many leading members—such as George Perkins, August Belmont, and Cyrus McCormick—favored unions in theory while resisting them in practice. In 1904 the NCF organized what was called a "welfare department" to assist businessmen in providing their workers with benefits that would keep them happy and out of unions—a technique pioneered by U.S. Steel and International Harvester. Gompers and other conservative union leaders stayed in the NCF anyway, no doubt because it allowed for informal contacts with big businessmen and because NCF members, if compelled to accept unions at all, always favored conservative ones.

The NCF campaigned for an easier antitrust policy and saw some of its views embodied in the Federal Trade Commission Act of 1914. It believed regulated monopoly was the best way to handle public utilities and helped get legislation passed to this effect in Wisconsin and elsewhere. It supported minimum wage laws because they prevented unscrupulous competitors from cutting costs by lowering wages. Under President Seth Low, former mayor of both Brooklyn and New York, and former president of Columbia, NCF membership rose from 1,500 in 1907 to 5,000 in 1912. NCF promoted compulsory mediation, as in the Newlands Act of 1913, supported timely reforms to head off radical agitation, and educated businessmen to the need for rationalizing and stabilizing industry through benevolent regulation. One of its most signal victories concerned workmen's compensation. Business leaders nearly all favored compensation, as an NCF survey discovered. The issue was whether workmen should be compensated by the states or by privately financed insurance programs. Business thought private insurance premiums would be too high and so favored state compensation. Labor believed benefits would be higher under private insurance plans. In the end Gompers was won over to the business view and, though delayed by the courts, workmen's compensation laws were enacted in every state but six by 1920.

Because Roosevelt shared so many of their views, NCF leaders, Perkins especially, were vital to his campaign, as were many younger members. Roosevelt also enjoyed the help of intellectuals like Herbert Croly. Croly was a journalist who had worked for many years on the *Architectural Record*. This experience might not seem to qualify a person for political analysis. But Croly was well informed, cared for the public interest, and believed that most reformers were trying to advance it in the wrong way. They wanted to revive competition and break the trusts; but the trusts, like the political bosses reformers also attacked, were holding the country together despite the fearful strains imposed by social and economic change. What was needed were federal regulation of business, repeal of the Sherman Act, and inheritance taxes to redistribute the national wealth. At the same time Croly believed that when a corporation grew so great that it became a "natural monopoly," the government should expropriate it—with compensation of course.

Unlike many NCF progressives, Croly favored the union shop. He also believed labor should receive the same help from government as business and be benevolently regulated in the same way. In his view muckraking would not help the country. Reform through a democratic elite, strong executive leadership, and the Republican party were answers to what ailed it. Croly's concept of democracy was paternalistic. He felt that his ideas, which he called the "New Nationalism," were in the line of descent from Alexander Hamilton, whereas crackbrained reformers had been misled by the Jefferson tradition. His nationalism, if aristocratic, was not racist, did not deify the state, and was not militaristic. The same could hardly be said of Roosevelt's "New Nationalism," although it did certainly owe something to Croly's influential book *The Promise of American Life* (1909), which had impressed many of Roosevelt's friends. TR already shared certain of Croly's views, though, and *The Promise of American Life* did not change his thinking so much as clarify it.

In 1910 at Osawatomie, Kans., Roosevelt expressed his new ideas as clearly as he ever would again. Part of his speech was the customary progressive fluff—down with the interests, up with the people, and so forth. He also called for the usual liberal and humanitarian reforms—direct primaries, tariff revision, an income tax, conservation, workmen's compensation, and protection for working women and children. But near the end he said that the American people demanded a New Nationalism which would put "the national need before sectional or personal advantage. It [the New Nationalism] is impatient of the utter confusion that results from local legislatures attempting to treat national issues as local issues. ... This New Nationalism regards the executive as the steward of the public welfare." And, TR went on, it "rightly maintains that every man holds his property subject to the general right of the community to regulate its use to whatever degree the public welfare may require." On the trusts he declared "combinations in industry are the result of an imperative economic law. ... The effort at prohibiting all combination has substantially failed. The way out lies, not in attempting to prevent such combinations, but in completely controlling them in the interest of the public welfare." This was hardly pure Crolyism. Roosevelt did not call for government support of unions. He also rejected Croly's argument that regulation by commission must fail. But the ideological match was close enough to make people think Croly had a great influence on TR. In 1912 Croly supported Roosevelt, as did such intellectuals as Walter Weyl and the brilliant young Walter Lippmann, who would join together in 1913 to found the *New Republic* magazine.

THE ELECTION OF 1912

These ideas, as expressed by Croly, and in a modified and more self-serving way by the National Civic Federation, were Roosevelt's best claim to another term in the White House. The problem was that to get there Roosevelt had to please another constituency with opposite values—the Midwestern Progressive insurgents and others who hated Taft but wanted to bust the trusts. The New Nationalists behind Roosevelt and the insurgents had much in common. They rejected laissez-faire, hoped to ease the class war through various reforms, admired efficiency and were de facto allies in the struggle against Republican old guardism. But much divided them as well. The insurgents were intensely hostile to the trusts. They believed in competition even though admitting the need to regulate it. Because they represented consumer interests they worked to keep prices down. Both groups favored regulation, but for different reasons. New Nationalists wanted to reduce competition; insurgents, to make big business observe higher standards of conduct. New Nationalists favored the administrative state, a powerful government able to rationalize business practices around the country; insurgents remained suspicious of big government even though their policies required government to expand. To guard against the bureaucratic state becoming a Frankenstein monster they promoted the instruments of direct democracy, thinking that such devices ensured that the people and not experts or special interests would have the last word.

Above all, each group defined the public interest in a different way. New Nationalists saw national well-being as a function of correct relationships between producer groups. Business, labor, and agriculture had distinctive aims, they held, which a strong government could orchestrate to the ultimate benefit of everyone. Insurgents believed in a mass politics that ignored producer orientations and united people in their roles as taxpayers and consumers. Where New Nationalists thought to organize government on an interest-group base, insurgents wanted a government that disdained interest groups in favor of a classless civic consciousness.

New Nationalists and insurgents were at odds on so many points that they would probably never have come together had it not been for their common enemy. But as the old guard was against Roosevelt he had to court the insurgents despite his numerous and important differences with them. At the same time Roosevelt ran the risk of becoming a purely insurgent candidate, thereby splitting the GOP. This did not bother Taft in the slightest. He said in a letter to a friend: "If I win the nomination and Roosevelt bolts, it means a long, hard fight and probably defeat. But I can stand defeat if we retain the regular Party as a nucleus of future conservative action." Defeat for Roosevelt, on the other hand, offered no compensations.

Roosevelt would probably have been better advised to wait until 1916, when the Republican convention would be open again. But four years was too long for such a restless spirit as his. As it happened, TR came surprisingly close to getting the GOP nomination anyway. Taft was not a good campaigner, as he showed by announcing that he would stand for reelection because "even a rat in a corner will fight." Roosevelt won enough primaries to make a good show at the convention. He needed about 70 more votes, and as perhaps 100 Taft delegates had dubious credentials he might have picked them up. But Taft controlled the credentials committee. The decisive moment came early when La Follette refused to let his 40-odd delegates go. If they had voted with Roosevelt's men to elect the temporary convention chairman, a contest Taft won 558 to 502, progressives might have gained control. Or if Roosevelt could have gotten 25 of the contested seats, he could have deadlocked the convention on its first ballot and probably won on a later vote. Thanks to La Follette, the Taft men were spared these dangers. La Follette accused Roosevelt of wrecking the progressive movement out of ambition, which was true in a sense. But La Follette wrecked it out of spite.

Roosevelt knew that an independent candidacy was hopeless. He launched one anyway, mostly because his followers were so taken with the idea that by not running he would have alienated them for good. No one attending the Progressive party convention that nominated Roosevelt seemed to care that defeat was certain. The delegates could hardly have been more enthusiastic. They sang spirited tunes like "Onward Christian Soldiers," in memory perhaps of TR's speech before the GOP convention, when he had said "we stand at Armageddon and we battle for the Lord." The Progressive convention went on to adopt the most advanced platform ever offered by a major party. It advocated all the usual instruments of direct democracy, plus a new one—the recall of judicial decisions—which Roosevelt was very keen on to the dismay of conservatives. The platform included a long series of welfare measures, called "industrial minimums," so comprehensive that leading social workers came over to Roosevelt almost en masse. Even Jane Addams, who loathed Roosevelt's militarism, became deeply involved in the campaign, a task made easier because the convention endorsed the limitation of naval armaments (had Roosevelt been elected, this resolution would instantly have become a dead letter). The platform also called for woman suffrage, a cause Roosevelt had no enthusiasm for at all.

Progressives divided sharply on the crucial matter of business regulation. A majority of the resolutions committee was for competition and wrote it into the platform. George Perkins, representing the New Nationalists, finally secured a version of the platform that said business concentration was "in some degree . . . inevitable and necessary." Roosevelt declared in his acceptance address that he was in favor of retaining the Sherman Act and making it more effective "where it is applied." Everyone seemed satisfied with this obscure formula, thus pointing up the dilemma facing Roosevelt. The Progressive party's unique feature was the New Nationalism, a creed that, to the degree they understood it, most Progressives were against. What they favored was the list of standard reforms making up most of the platform. This list was admirably complete, but since Woodrow Wilson was not against many of these reforms, their inclusion in the platform gave progressive Democrats little reason to bolt their party. As there was little popular support for the New Nationalism Roosevelt was obliged to dilute it. Some New Nationalists had hoped for a great debate that would set the Hamiltonian philosophy of Roosevelt against Wilson's allegedly Jeffersonian faith. They were to be disappointed.

As the campaign wore on it became evident that Taft was the only candidate calling for support of the status quo; Roosevelt and Wilson alike appealed to the desire for change. Roosevelt blurred his stand on the trusts. Wilson softened his opposition to them, announcing that he favored "reasonable" combinations. "Business," he declared, "underlies everything in our national life, including our spiritual life." No one who cared for America would "wish to upset business or interfere with any honest and natural process of it." The advantages of scale in business were obvious. It was "plain enough that we cannot go back to the old competitive system under which individuals were the competitors." Competition could not be established by law against the drift of worldwide economic tendencies, and business done on a large scale by a single organization was not "necessarily dangerous to the liberties, even the economic liberties, of a great people like our own." Where Wilson did criticize combinations it was for particular reasons. He was against U.S. Steel because so much of its stock had been water. He left International Harvester alone, even though it produced 80 to 90 percent of all harvesting machines, because its stock was sound—perhaps also because Cyrus McCormick had contributed generously to his campaign.

Wilson's flexibility was the last blow to Roosevelt's campaign. TR split the Republican vote without attracting large numbers of Democrats. Big business did not rally behind him as expected, even though angry at Taft. Corporate leaders who had enjoyed a long and profit-able association with the GOP were not about to change parties overnight, especially when the new party had such uncertain pros-pects. Most businessmen were not New Nationalists and so not attracted by TR's vision of the good society. They distrusted the Progressive party because it attracted nearly every independent in the country, many of them quite unsafe by business standards. Roosevelt himself later called them "the lunatic fringe." Since Wil-son was clearly a reliable man with capitalist supporters of his own, business was not frightened of him, as it had been of Bryan years before. TR had enough money to campaign on, thanks to Perkins, Frank Munsey the publisher, and other wealthy supporters. Even so, his party—being brand-new, almost entirely middle class, and organized from the top down wholly on national issues—lacked the roots to endure. Roosevelt won over four million votes, more than Taft got and only about two million fewer than were cast for Wilson. But the Progressive party elected only a handful of people to office.

Progressives were undiscouraged. No sensible person expected a new party to win many elections the first time around. The social workers and reformers especially began planning almost at once for 1914 and 1916. Roosevelt did not. Like the professional politician he was, TR privately advised a friend to rejoin the GOP. "There are no loaves and fishes," he observed. Without patronage to dispense the new party had to fail. All the same, enthusiasm remained so high in the Progressive party that it took four years for Roosevelt to kill it. By that time the old guard was solidly in control of the GOP. What had begun as a crusade to push the GOP left ended by driving it to the right.

BIBLIOGRAPHICAL NOTES

In addition to the books noted in the two earlier chapters, these have been useful here. Even though I disagree with much of it, Richard Hofstadter, *The Age of Reform* (1955), is so rich and stimulating that every student should read it. A good, conventional survey of the period 1900–12 is George E. Mowry, *The Era of Theodore Roosevelt* (1958). An excellent brief analysis is John Morton Blum, *The Republican Roosevelt* (1954). The standard biog-raphy is Henry F. Pringle, *Life and Times of William Howard Taft* (2 vols.,

1939). Though written for partisan reasons Robert M. La Follette, *La Follette's Autobiography* (1913) is still interesting. There are some revealing documents in Robert S. Maxwell, ed., *La Follette* (1969). An important article charging that historians have neglected labor's role in Progressive reform is Joseph J. Huthmacher, "Urban Liberalism and the Age of Reform," *Mississippi Valley Historical Review* (September, 1962). Samuel P. Hays, "The Politics of Reform in Municipal Government in the Progressive Era," *Pacific Northwest Quarterly* (1964), focuses on Pittsburgh but has much broader implications. Charles Forcey, *The Crossroads of Liberalism: Croly, Weyl, Lippmann, and the Progressive Era, 1900–1925* (1961), is a penetrating intellectual history.

4

REVOLUTIONARIES AND REFORMERS

Americans are a great people for nostrums—Fourierism and hydropathy in the 1840s, Maoism and organic foods in the 1960s. No age has been free of them; some, like the Progressive era, have been richly endowed. Especially large numbers of people were drawn to social movements in these years, proportionately more than at any time since, thanks particularly to the Socialist party, which at its peak attracted 6 percent of the popular vote. If America had been more like other industrial countries, the Socialist party would have become a great force in American life. Because it did not, most histories pass over the SP quickly. Just another failed enthusiasm, they imply, which is true in a sense. But that socialism withered is itself a crucial fact. Usually a movement's significance is measured by its power. American socialism is important precisely because it never acquired any.

THE SOCIALIST PARTY

At the turn of the century socialism was rising in all great industrial countries. The British Labour party had two members of Parliament in 1900, 50 in 1906. By 1914 there were 76 Socialist deputies in the French Chamber. In 1912 German Social Democrats held 110 seats in the Reichstag, where they were the largest single party. Socialism lagged behind in America, but not by very much. Though only six years old in 1907, the party had organizations in 39 states and sponsored 50 publications. In 1908 it had 40,000 members in 3,000 locals. It published 100 newspapers, notably the *Appeal to Reason*, which spoke for socialism in the language of Populism and had a circulation of 350,000, mainly in the Middle and Far West. *Wilshire's Magazine* printed 270,000 copies a month. In New York the *Call* preached socialism in English every day, as did the *Jewish Daily Forward* in Yiddish.

For his presidential campaign in 1908 Socialist candidate Eugene V. Debs chartered a train, the Red Special. Democrats charged it was financed with Republican money. The SP replied by publishing a list of 20,000 people who had paid for the charter. When accused of being foreigners Socialists could show that 70 percent of all party members were native-born. In 1910 Milwaukee elected a Socialist mayor and sent Victor Berger to Congress, as New York's Lower East Side would send Meyer London in 1915. By 1912 something like 1,000 Socialists held public office in 33 states and 160 cities; there were 118,000 dues-paying members of the party. In that year Debs won 897,000 votes for president. The party sponsored hundreds of publications; hundreds more used material furnished by party headquarters. The *Appeal* had increased its circulation to 500,000. The *Jewish Daily Forward* was moving toward a peak of 250,000 subscribers.

Party strength was not measured by voters and readers alone. The SP had great intellectual and artistic resources as well. The Intercollegiate Socialist Society, for instance, worked with students. The Rand School of Social Science in New York trained organizers. The *International Socialist Review* discussed issues and strategy on a high intellectual plane. The *Masses*—which combined socialism with ashcan art, free love, feminism, and good times—was America's most lively and original publication. The SP attracted writers and artists like Max Eastman, Walter Lippmann, John Reed, Stuart Davidson, Boardman Robinson, and John Sloan. If talent meant as much as votes the SP would have beaten the major parties easily. But in fact 1912 was its best year. In 1913 "Big Bill" Haywood, the Wobbly leader, was expelled from the party's national executive committee for seeming to condone violence, a burning issue among leftists then, as in the 1960s. By 1914 the party had lost 50,000 members. In 1917 it was repressed for opposing American entry into World War I. The SP never recovered from these events.

The conventional wisdom has it that socialism failed because it was un-American, and, after the rise of people's capitalism, irrelevant. Yet it was very American. Party membership in relation to registered voters was highest in Oklahoma, where there were few immigrants. Not until after the Russian Revolution, by which time the SP was already in retreat, did immigrants constitute a majority. Socialism was no more irrelevant in America than in England. Both countries were rich and great. Both suffered from poverty, social injustice, and the maldistribution of wealth. Yet in one country socialism flourished while in the other it died. This cannot be explained on the grounds that America offered unique opportunities for working people. Upward mobility seems to have been no greater in America than in other industrial countries at the same stage of development.

Often socialism's decline in America is attributed to factionalism and bad strategy. The right wing, composed of what leftists contemptuously called "sewer Socialists," was too much concerned with municipal ownership of public utilities and other tepid reforms. As the right wing never offered a truly radical alternative to the existing parties there was never much reason to vote for it. The left wing, in contrast, was too noisy and militant; it spoke of revolution and supported the Wobblies. Leftists frightened the middle class, while failing to offer workers tangible benefits. Until 1913, though, coexistence was possible because while the right had the power, the left had the glory: rightists controlled most party institutions; leftists supplied moral energy, vision, and Gene Debs, the SP's most beloved and charismatic figure. To say that both sides had failings is also to say that they needed each other. When the right wing expelled Haywood and drove many leftists out of the party it foreclosed its own future. Even when it was wrong, the left's vigor, intelligence, and appeal to free spirits made it essential. Without a left wing the party no longer stood for much that was calculated to inspire high feelings.

Factionalism alone was not to blame for the SP's failure. All parties have factions; viable ones stay together despite them. Perhaps the chief reason for this is that power, or even the prospect of it, depends on unity. To put doctrine ahead of party interests is to admit, however unwittingly, that victory is not expected. In driving out leftists, conservative Socialists indicated they would rather be right than president, which was to say no hope remained to them of the SP becoming a major party. Leftists, by abandoning the SP, said the same thing. The party split was a confession of failure, not the cause of it.

Socialism collapsed in the United States because it was unable to recruit working people in sufficient numbers. English socialism rose solidly from a trade union base, hence the name British Labour party. In America not many unions were Socialist. The majority were apolitical. Trade unionists rejected the idea of a class struggle, relying on the self-interest of skilled workers to better conditions and on management to bake ever larger pies for both sides to cut up. Union leaders, notably Gompers himself, hated socialism as much as any capitalist did, more so in a way because trade unionists and Socialists both hoped to attract the same men. At first Socialists were not discouraged when few workers joined them. They believed that in time workers would acquire class consciousness and reject business unionism. But the workers never did.

This seems mainly to have been on account of immigration. In the forty years before 1900 about 14,000,000 immigrants, many of them English-speaking, arrived in America. During the next fifteen years about 14.5 million poured in, mostly from eastern and southern Europe. The new immigration renewed nativist sentiments. It made native-born workers fear for their jobs, or at least for their income levels, which floods of cheap labor were thought to depress. They despaired of organizing unskilled workers who could not even speak English. For their part immigrants brought over their national and religious prejudices, making it easy for employers to play off one group against another. Most had come to this country to make money, not to join unions or political organizations. Only the Industrial Workers of the World succeeded in organizing multinational work forces, and then seldom and for short periods only. Where workers were so divided there could be no class consciousness. Without class consciousness there could not be a fully organized proletariat, still less a Socialist one.

Socialists thus faced an insoluble dilemma. Skilled workers preferred trade unions to socialism. They often identified with the middle class. Unskilled workers could not be organized by anyone except the IWW; and then not for long. Socialists tried many tactics to solve these problems, none of which worked well. Leftists attacked the AFL and flirted with dual unionism (that is building rival unions like the IWW). Rightists favored working within the AFL and hedging on immigration. The left's tactics alienated trade unionists. The right's compromises violated the spirit of socialism even while nominally promoting it and did not work anyway.

Both sides were not so much wrong as helpless. Dual unionism made no sense because the AFL had already organized most workers who were capable of being organized at the time. Yet boring from within the AFL was difficult too because skilled workers did not look beyond their immediate self-interest and felt adequately served by their conservative leaders. Perhaps Socialists could have tried to outbid AFL officers, beating them at their own game by offering greater benefits to skilled workers. But this would have meant compromising the interests of the working class as a whole. Socialism perished accordingly, and with it the best hope of finding an alternative to corporate capitalism.

Socialists assumed that workers would become aware of their collective oppression and unite to end it. But the sense of what divided them was stronger among American workers than any awareness of what they had in common. Middle-class people disagreed with each other, but were less fragmented. They were mostly native-born WASPs to start with. And when the middle class grew it did so by assimilation. To become middle class meant as a rule to accept the core values of bourgeois culture—law and order, the work ethic, self-help, faith in progress and education. Lower-class growth came through immigration, but more numbers did not mean more power because of competition for jobs and increased discrimination. Meanwhile, as the middle class grew in size it grew in strength. The primacy of bourgeois values led even many workers to accept them. Debs said that he would rise with his class, not above it. This was an uncommon view. Most workers meant to advance by their own efforts or, if not, to give their children a leg up. As the class structure was relatively porous this was not impossibly hard to do. Upward mobility made the middle classes strong. The only effective class consciousness in America was middle-class consciousness, hence the failure of socialism in this country even as it flourished elsewhere.

In the long run, however, socialism withered in all the Western industrial states. Britain, Germany, Sweden, and other nations have been at times governed by parties which once were Socialist and still invoke their militant traditions now and again. But in practice the Social Democratic parties have been hardly more radical than their frankly capitalistic opponents. Socialism, which once stood for revolution, now in developed states means only capitalism plus social welfare. The difference between the countries of western and northern Europe and the United States is simply that their social welfare benefits are, in relation to national wealth, better than ours. This is no small thing, even though much less than Socialists had anticipated.

ANARCHISM

Socialism hardly exhausted the list of radical alternatives during the Progressive era. People could choose among three kinds of anarchism alone. One was domestic in origin and held that the good society would be utterly without government or limits to enterprise. It trusted the working of natural laws to maintain equity among men. This carried laissez-faire to a point beyond which most of its advocates were willing to go. Yet the idea never died out and finds expression today among the followers of Ayn Rand. What could be more American than to combine hatred of the state with a love of enterprise? And as the state fought ever more costly wars, while it helped big business flourish at the expense of small business, what could be more logical? But Americans, though often sensible, are seldom logical, hence their distrust of this kind of reasoning.

More significant in its time was European anarchism, brought to the United States chiefly by German, Italian, and Jewish immigrants. It never acquired many followers either, even though it inspired fears all out of proportion to its size. This was because a handful of anarchists in this group believed in the "propaganda of the deed," holding that acts of terror would catalyze revolutionary sentiments and overturn the state. The propaganda of the deed would have been a pathetic notion were it not destructive. Anarchists committed few outrages in America from the 1880s to World War I, fewer perhaps than in the 1960s, but they had terrible consequences. Someone threw a bomb at policemen during a Chicago anarchist rally in 1886, killing seven and wounding seventy others. In reprisal eight anarchist leaders were arbitrarily arrested and convicted of inciting the unknown bomber. Four were hanged; one comitted suicide; and the rest went to prison. The anarchist movement of the day was broken. Though anything but anarchistic, the Knights of Labor were also severely damaged by the backlash.

In 1892 a pair of young anarchists, Emma Goldman and Alexander Berkman, conspired to assassinate Henry Clay Frick for having crushed the steelworkers union at Carnegie's Homestead (Pa.) works. Frick was only slightly injured, but Berkman went to prison for many years and anarchists were rousted all over the country. In 1901 a deranged young person named Leon Czolgosz shot President McKinley to death. Once again anarchists everywhere came under attack. John Most, the aging dean of anarchism, was sent to jail for having reprinted an old treatise on political assassination shortly before McKinley's death. By this time Goldman and Berkman had repudiated the propaganda of the deed because they had come to believe it was meaningless in a country where there was oppression but no despotism. Emma Goldman, who defended Czolgosz, told reporters that she would be glad to nurse McKinley were that possible. He was a human being, even though of the wrong political faith. This change of heart came too late. Anarchism was thoroughly discredited and, while it never died out, it never had political significance again either, except as an excuse for repression.

A third strain of anarchism, called "anarcho-syndicalism," enjoyed more influence because it was espoused by Wobblies, as members of the Industrial Workers of the World were called. The IWW was formed in 1905 by Daniel DeLeon, Bill Haywood of the Western Federation of Miners, and others to unite all unorganized workers in one big union, as the Knights of Labor had tried to do earlier. Unlike the Knights, the Wobblies were anticapitalist and also antipolitical. Members did not vote but organized workers in hopes of someday seizing control of industry. It was never entirely clear how this would happen, or what would follow if it did. Syndicalists hoped vaguely that people would be organized at their places of work, making other forms of government unnecessary. In the event, their want of theory made little difference since the Wobblies were smashed during World War I.

But even before then the IWW had developed fatal contradictions. Wobblies did not believe in business unionism, the daily tasks of bargaining with management, safeguarding gains, and the like. And they disdained political action. The result was that while they could win strikes—notably at Lawrence, Mass., in 1912—they could not build on them. Without political connections and without the benefits that bound workers to conventional unions, the IWW could offer members no reason to stay on once a strike was done. Yet to compromise in these ways would have been to give up the principles that made the organization unique. There being no way out of this impasse the Wobblies succumbed, much like the Socialists, first to attrition, after 1917 to repression. Later the CIO would take the principle of industrial unionism, which the IWW pioneered, and by annexing it to business unionism would organize the mass production industries. Wobblies could not have done this, but neither did they want to. Their folly was also their glory, as with so many other radicals.

BOURGEOIS RADICALISM

Middle-class radicals had their own panaceas, such as nationalism and the single tax. Nationalists, followers of Edward Bellamy, who had written a fabulously popular utopian novel called *Looking Backward* in 1888, advocated a kind of benevolent state socialism. Single taxers, inspired by Henry George's powerful tract *Progress and Poverty* (1879), believed that unearned profit from land ownership was America's curse. They proposed to abolish it by a single tax on undeveloped property, which would eliminate unearned income and provide enough money for the state to meet pressing social needs, thus making other forms of taxation unnecessary. Some middle-class radicals supported the Socialist party, or proclaimed themselves to be "philosophical anarchists," a term devised apparently to imply that they were not to be taken seriously as real anarchists were. None of these movements amounted to much. Collectively they were important in that middle-class radicals contributed also to the general buoyancy and hopefulness of the age. They also contributed time and sometimes money to more humble reforms, on the admirable theory that today's victims ought not to be sacrificed to tomorrow's hopes.

HUMANITARIAN REFORM

New Nationalists, municipal reformers, and others concerned with efficiency and stability all considered themselves progressive, and so they were. But they were hard-liners when it came to social change. What interested them were things like management, structure, process. But the reformers posterity most admires worked the soft side, the human side, of change in their time. Few care to read now about the movement for municipally owned utilities; few can help being moved by the fight against child labor.

Social justice was never more ardently desired than in the Progressive era, and perhaps never before had people sought it in such varied ways. Radicals had a passion for it, but so did liberals such as Jane Addams, Lillian Wald, Florence Kelley, Paul Kellogg, Owen Lovejoy, and hundreds more. Behind these leaders were tens of thousands all over the country who sought to help poor and oppressed people. Often they did so out of pity. Florence Kelley, though a Socialist, felt that compassion was the chief reason why upper-class women supported the National Consumers' League's efforts to aid working girls. Some women were drawn to social work because it gave them rewarding employment of a sort largely denied them elsewhere. These were emotional reasons, but the logic of self-interest applied too. If one wanted, as middle-class people did, a healthy, prosperous, and contented society, gross inequities could not be tolerated. It was generous to spend time helping the unfortunate. It was common sense too. Social order depended, to a degree anyway, on social justice—a point grasped early by farsighted conservatives such as Chancellor Bismarck of Germany. Americans were slower to realize this, maybe because blinded by social Darwinism. In any event, by the early twentieth century it was understood that punitive measures alone would never bring peace.

Social justice people were less concerned with theory than fact. They saw suffering around them and did what they could to ease it. But they were iimited too, like New Nationalists, though in a somewhat different way. New Nationalists conceded labor's right to collective bargaining, while refusing to bargain collectively. Humanitarians saw the need for social justice, but would not pay the price for it. Although socialism was a logical way to achieve equity, it was overwhelmingly rejected by middle-class Americans. Religious people were repelled by its materialism, despite the efforts of Christian Socialists to make Marx and Jesus compatible. Some, like Jane Addams, who were really Socialists at heart, stopped short of open conversion because Socialists believed in the class struggle. Jane Addams knew it existed, but she refused to recognize it officially. Her mission was to promote peace, brotherhood, and community —all of which she thought Socialists were hostile to. Socialists tried in vain to persuade her that under socialism there would be a wider fellowship than was possible in a bourgeois state. For most reformers socialism remained the evil that, by overhauling capitalism, they hoped to avert.

Having rejected socialism, it might be supposed that middle-class reformers would have taken the next most logical step and supported trade unions. Poor people in the Progressive era were nearly always employed, in fact overemployed, for in many families everyone worked long hours, regardless of age. Unskilled workers were seldom able to help themselves. Few unions took an interest in them. Although this created a vacuum into which reformers might have moved, except for settlement house residents only a small number did.

Lacking grand strategies for reform, well-intentioned middle-class persons were obliged to see each problem as unique and in need of a solution peculiar to itself. This open-mindedness was not without charm. It had, however, the drawback of leaving nearly all problems unsolved. Housing reformers worked on housing, child labor crusaders attacked child labor, and so it went. Each group did some good; none was strong enough to cure the evils it attacked. Even had the groups been stronger most problems could not be solved on a piecemeal basis. Laws could be passed abolishing child labor. They could not abolish the needs that drove children into mills. Laws were passed to make housing safer and healthier. This did not really help the poor, who could not afford the higher rents made necessary by higher standards. The central problem of the time was that a majority of working-class families lived in poverty even when fully employed. This being so, a housing project here, a nursing service there, were not going to make much difference. Even ambitious social legislation, such as the minimum wage and maximum hour laws for working women, helped very little. Desperate situations require strong remedies. But humanitarian reformers had rejected comprehensive solutions in favor of piecemeal reforms. This insured that they would fail to build a just society, however much good they did.

Though viewing each problem separately, humanitarian reformers attacked them in similar ways. Once roused by a muckraker or inspiring speaker, humanitarians, as might have been expected in a bureaucratic age, formed organizations. There were hundreds, perhaps thousands, of these on every level of government, the altruistic counterparts of those other organizations through which the middle classes promoted their own interests. Humanitarian bodies generally possessed the following traits. Nearly all relied on a mixture of private benevolence and public support. Most reformers began by investigating and publicizing abuses and ended by promoting legislation to correct them. Most moved from amateurism to professionalism, often very quickly. The model for this transformation was charity work, which after the Civil War relied mainly on volunteers, called "friendly visitors," in dealing with the poor, but by the turn of the century was becoming professionalized. At the same time, urban philanthropic bodies were joining together in professionally led charity organization societies to coordinate their scattered efforts. The tendency toward professionalization and bureaucratization took place even among people who were opposed to them in principle, as settlement houses demonstrated.

Settlement houses were established, mainly by women, to put middle-class people directly in touch with the poor. The theory was that poor people needed helpful neighbors, not "friendly visitors" who, however friendly, had the power to give or deny aid and so could never deal with clients on anything like an equal basis. Settlement residents meant to help poor immigrants by living with them, learning their needs, and distributing the fruits of the resident's superior American experience and education.

If this was patronizing, it was not meant to be. Residents tried to appreciate ethnic traits that ran contrary to their own tastes and values. Often this did not go beyond celebrating folk culture. At a time when everyone wanted to change immigrants into WASPs even this was something. What settlement residents wanted to promote most of all was community. They meant their houses to be rallying points in the urban wilderness, where neighbors would plan and labor together for mutual benefit. But the settlement ethic and the settlement house were at odds with each other. The ethic held that neighbors could help themselves; the house proclaimed that they could not. If neighborhoods were as self-sufficient as residents claimed, they could have built their own community centers.

Settlement houses did a great deal of good, mostly at the expense of doctrine. Residents were supposed to be volunteers, as at first they were. But after World War I more and more of them were paid professionals. Residents were also supposed to be neighbors. Yet most settlement residents did not stay in the neighborhood long. Later, when they became professionals, many lived elsewhere and only worked in the neighborhood. Settlements offered social services chiefly to support fraternity and the communal ethic. But in time social services became their whole reason for being and the ethic disappeared.

Settlements vividly demonstrated the progressive compulsion to translate morality into institutions. In the world's eyes settlement houses were very successful, as evidenced by their multi-million dollar plants and elaborate programs. In their hearts some founders must have had doubts. For the purpose of the settlement had not been to build greatly, nor even to feed and teach and organize, as was done so well. Their special mission was to link neighbor with neighbor, to build great communities so that the worst parts of the cities might become the best. There is a special irony in the fact that the settlements were undone by success, whereas so many other movements perished of failure.

The best settlements were great anyway. They provided meeting rooms and sometimes organizers for labor unions. A few, like Hull House and the University Settlement in New York, were proving grounds where all kinds of reformers did their basic training. Some, like Chicago Commons and the Northwestern University Settlement, sponsored reform slates that beat local bosses. Henry Street

Settlement gave New York its first public visiting nurse service. The Music Settlement in New York turned ghetto youngsters into professional musicians. Where other reformers were interested in one or two causes, settlements were interested in everything. At times they rarely did any one thing so well as the specialists, which was why in the end most concentrated on youth problems. But because they cast their nets so broadly they were at first centers of enlightenment that drew on the best talents of their age. It is difficult to imagine what progressives would have done without them.

IMMIGRATION

Settlements were located in immigrant quarters for the most part. After business concentration and political reform, immigration was the problem Americans were most anxious about. In fact, immigration was not itself the problem, though few seemed to know this. America was short of labor and immigrants poured in because there was work for them. It was often cruelly hard work, but not necessarily worse than they were used to and generally better paying. And it often carried the hope of advancement for the second generation if not the first. If foreign workers held wages down it was partly because unions refused to organize them. The union solution to immigration was to restrict it. This was hardly better than the union solution to the problem of working women, which was nonexistent. Unskilled women also drove wages down, perhaps even more than immigrant men. But most trade union leaders ignored women, where they did not actively discriminate against them. Through most of the period businessmen favored immigration precisely because foreigners worked cheap. But they also complained of the immigrant problem, though it was chiefly a matter of the low wages business paid, rather than of foreign origin or parentage. If the ghettos were dirty, crime-infested, unhealthy, it was because immigrants were poor and had little political power. Yet immigrants were held in contempt by the very people who exploited them and condemned for following machine politicians when in most places only the bosses met any of their needs.

Because the immigrant problem was an income problem it tended to solve itself. As the GNP rose so, haltingly, did incomes. The children of immigrants went to decent public schools in most cities, learned English and, as a rule, did better than their parents. The minute they could afford to, immigrants moved out of the tenements, sometimes en masse, to form newer, better enclaves elsewhere. They did not melt together as expected. But they floated upward all the same. In 1892, 75 percent of New York's Jews lived on the Lower East Side, then the most congested residential district in the world (more so even than Bombay, India, which was famous for overcrowding). By 1916 only 23 percent of New York's Jewry remained there. Jews were more successful than other large ethnic groups, but what they did others did also, if more slowly.

Because immigration was a continuous process until World War I it was hard for native Americans to see that it posed few long-term problems. Older and second-generation ethnics were rising even before 1914, but newcomers kept filling in the bottom ranks. This inspired a new nativism that was as virulent as before, and even more effective. Union pressure on Congress grew. A·sophisticated racist ideology was developed, notably by Madison Grant, who in *The Passing of the Great Race* (1916) invoked anthropology to show that Teutons were superior to the Alpine and Mediterranean "races." This seemed to put nativism on a scientific basis. In 1913 and 1915 Congress passed bills restricting immigration to literate persons, though in each case presidential vetos, narrowly sustained, bought time. In 1917 time ran out. Inflamed by patriotism, Congress enacted a literacy test. More severe and effective restrictions followed after the war.

CIVIL RIGHTS

The problems of immigrants were less serious than those of blacks, although not many humanitarians seemed aware of the fact. This was in part a matter of visibility. Immigrants flooded the cities and a knowledge of them was inescapable. But there were very few blacks outside the South. Overt discrimination was so universal that hardly anyone in the Progressive era noticed it. Nearly all Americans were racist, though outside the South prejudice was not so much conscious as atmospheric. Everyone took the condition of blacks for granted. The results of discrimination seemed to justify the practice of it. Those few who wished to do something about racism faced staggering difficulties. In 1904, when Mary White Ovington, later a founder of the NAACP, organized a large interracial dinner, nearly every newspaper in New York attacked her.

The mere existence of the National Association for the Advancement of Colored People was a thing of wonder. Race had been a great issue until after the Civil War, but by the end of the century it was considered solved. Northerners had tired of sectional conflict and wanted national unity. To achieve it meant accepting southern views on the race question, or at least conceding that the racial issue was a sectional and not a national one, to be resolved by southerners alone. This became all the easier to swallow when American colonialism was justified on the grounds that whites could rule colored people better than such people could govern themselves, which was what southern whites had always said. Once the United States took this line in the Philippines it was difficult to argue that it was true in the islands, but not in the South.

Accommodation was made easier by Booker T. Washington, president of the Tuskegee Institute in Alabama. Since segregation and discrimination were so deeply rooted in the South, Washington argued that blacks should accept it as a fact of life and concentrate on self-advancement. By accepting social segregation and political disenfranchisement, Washington thought blacks might gain, or be allowed, economic opportunity. At Tuskegee he trained young black men and women to become craftsmen and small proprietors, not professionals. Later generations would criticize Washington for selling out. Tuskegee had flourished, it would be said, at the expense of black hopes elsewhere. Perhaps Washington only did what he had to. Blacks were in no position to fight for themselves. Conciliation might well succeed where protest had failed, and in any case there seemed no other choice.

But the truth was that except for attracting white philanthropists, Tuskegeeism did not work. Washington preached submission during the 1890s, yet lynchings increased, averaging 187.5 a year throughout the decade. The lynch rate fell thereafter as economic conditions improved, but also as fewer whites were killed. In the 1890s over 32 percent of all lynching victims were white. In the next decade they were less than 12 percent. Thus, while fewer people were lynched, this did not help blacks because they were being killed almost as frequently as before. Nor did Tuskegeeism keep segregation from becoming more rigid. Between 1900 and 1911 ten southern states elaborated their segregation laws, and in 1913 a movement began in North Carolina to segregate farmland. All this was not Washington's fault, but it cast doubt on the value of collaborating with white authorities. Moreover, Washington used his influence to bar alternatives. He had almost a veto power over philanthropic contributions to blacks and denied funds to his critics. He especially disliked the charge that by funneling blacks into industrial education (as his program, which stressed crafts like bricklaying, was wrongly called) he was keeping talented people down.

In 1903 W. E. B. DuBois, a Harvard Ph.D., published *The Souls of Black Folk* and quickly became the best known of Washington's black rivals. Instead of industrial education he favored cultivating a black elite, "the talented tenth," who would lead blacks to freedom. In 1910 when the NAACP was organized, DuBois became its director of research and publications, thus gaining a regular outlet for his views. In its early days the NAACP had little weight and only a tiny voice, the magazine *Crisis* which DuBois edited. *Crisis* in principle demanded freedom, equality, and power for blacks, just as militants do today. But in practice lynching remained the great evil NAACP leaders had to contend with. They could not prevent lynchings or see that the guilty were prosecuted afterwards. Some lynchings were announced in advance and special trains chartered so that all who wished could see them. Occasionally pictures of the mob and its victim were circulated on postcards. In such a climate there was little hope of justice. Demagogues like Tom Watson of Georgia and Ben Tillman of South Carolina toured the Chautauqua circuit, pouring out racist abuse from the very platforms which, on another day, William Jennings Bryan or William James might occupy. Popular books like *The Clansman* (which became D.W. Griffith's masterpiece *Birth of a Nation*) glorified the Ku Klux Klan. Worse than the popular books were the supposedly scientific works that showed Negroid brains to be inferior to Caucasian. Even such reputable social scientists as E. A. Ross of the University of Wisconsin believed this. Given this climate of thought, it was inevitable that racial violence would move North if many blacks did. When World War I cut off the immigration from Europe blacks came North in larger numbers than at any earlier time and terrible race riots followed, notably in East St. Louis during the war and in Chicago just afterwards. There was little progress for blacks in the Progressive era.

FEMINISM

Women had a more complex and positive experience. In the early nineteenth century they had few rights in law, fewer still by custom. They were denied access to higher education and all interesting occupations. Middle-class women were allowed to teach, sometimes. Lower-class women did unskilled work as domestics and factory hands. Middle-class women were supposedly reconciled to their narrow role by an ethic which held that, while good for little outside the home, they were exactly fitted for what had to be done within it. Besides having a special gift for housework they were very moral, hence perfectly suited to raising children, and sometimes even the ethical standards of husbands. The problem was that since men had a monopoly of vice, and most women of virtue, there was little a good woman could do with a man except be degraded by him. As the only proper companions for women were other women, they came together socially, especially in church work, which became, as society grew more secular, an increasingly feminine sphere. They also formed clubs and societies directed at suitable problems like child welfare and the "fallen woman."

A small minority of women rebelled against their condition with modest results. By the 1880s a fair number had gained access to higher education and sometimes even the professions, notably teaching, nursing, and library work. Organized feminists were never numerous, but they promoted some legal reforms and made the oppression of women a little more difficult than it had been earlier. More important, the growth of a female leisure class led to a great proliferation of women's clubs, temperance societies, and moral purity associations directed against the double standard of morals and against prostitution. Most of these enterprises were not feminist in any obvious way. Some were antifeminist, insisting that women wanted only to stay in the home, but were kept from doing so by male neglect of important problems.

As men became better organized in the 1890s and thereafter, women did also, both in broader groups such as the General Federation of Woman's Clubs and the Women's Christian Temperance Union, as well as in more specialized bodies like the National Woman's Trade Union League, the National Consumers' League, the Association of Collegiate Alumnae (later the American Association of University Women), and many other organizations. At the same time the proportion of women who worked, mostly at menial jobs, increased.

By the Progressive era there were five main categories of women with a claim on the public's attention: a handful of outright feminists; a larger number of "social feminists," who favored women's rights but were more deeply involved in other reforms; a still larger group of well-intentioned leisure-class women who sought outlets in clubs, temperance societies, and the like; a substantial number of women who were discriminated against as professionals; and the mass of working women who had little consciousness of their objective condition but needed help all the same. Each of these fared somewhat differently.

Ordinary working women, even more than workingmen, were unable to do much for themselves. They were ignored by unions because they were mostly unskilled and because men resented them. One union leader admitted that it was not "economic" to recruit working women and children because even when unionized the dues they paid, based on their low wages, did not equal the cost of organizing them. This was business unionism with a vengeance. A few middle-class groups like the National Consumers' League and the Woman's Trade Union League tried to help women from the outside, but without great success. Most reformers thought the best way to help them was through minimum wage and maximum hour laws. A fair number of these were passed by the states to much applause. But before long women were complaining that restrictions kept them from getting the best jobs, which often involved night work, long hours, or some other requirement denied them by law. They also asked why the AFL favored protective legislation for women workers but not for men. The answer was that the AFL believed men could do better through collective bargaining than by legislation. The women who knew this felt that what was true for male workers would be true for females, if only unions cared to organize them. But as they did not, women had no choice but to take what they could get, little as it was.

Higher-status employed women were not strikingly more effective, even though better organized. The Association of Collegiate Alumnae, which consisted mainly of teachers, spent most of its time rating colleges and universities according to their degree of excellence and treatment of women. This was a harmless exercise, but it did nothing for women teachers. Other professionals established women's medical societies and similar organizations. These accomplished little because there was no force behind them. The condition of professional and skilled working women would not change for many years.

The other three categories did somewhat better. Leisure-class women, who had begun serious organizing in the 1890s, often were politicized by experience. The General Federation of Women's Clubs, probably their most important outlet, campaigned for pure food and drug laws, conservation, higher age of consent laws, and other reforms. To a degree, clubwomen and prohibitionists allied themselves with social feminists, especially where the interests of working women and children were concerned. Social feminism thus acquired a wider base. Many women accepted Jane Addams's law, which held that pure homes required a pure environment. Accordingly, it was the housewife's duty to reform whatever menaced her home. If not literally true, this argument enabled women to retain their traditional image as domestic beings, while at the same time transcending it. Great numbers of women did so, frightening politicians, who could not be certain what the real power of women was, or how many male voters they influenced.

This emergence of middle-class women provided feminists for the first time with a large constituency. The early feminists had come to women's rights through the back door. They mainly wanted prohibition or the end of slavery, but were handicapped by male opposition to women entering public life. Originally demanding their rights in the name of justice, the growing interest of women in social reform provided them with a more potent argument: that without the vote women could never be effective reformers. This raised the back door approach nearly to the level of principle, but was probably not true. Women were no more powerful in the 1920s than they had been earlier, despite the franchise. It was a plausible argument all the same and after 1912 became generally accepted.

In the next few years everything changed. Where once feminists were numbered in the thousands, they soon numbered in the millions. This growth was triggered by a handful of women under the leadership of a young Quaker named Alice Paul, a social worker who went to England for advanced study. She was converted to militancy by Emmeline Pankhurst who, disdaining the orderly methods of other suffragists, had turned to direct action. Those who followed Mrs. Pankhurst (disparagingly called "suffragettes," a term they embraced, thus reducing its value as an epithet) demonstrated even when it was illegal. If arrested they went on hunger strikes and had to be force-fed, to the public's dismay. When released they went in for sabotage and arson, which also upset the public. Suffragettes burned down Lloyd George's house, mutilated works of art, fired rifles at railway locomotives, and violated mailboxes.

Miss Paul came home convinced that suffragette tactics would lead to a federal amendment enfranchising women. At the time all campaigns for equal suffrage were aimed at the states, the constitutional amendment tactic having languished for years. With a few followers she went to Washington and organized a suffragist demonstration to coincide with President Wilson's inauguration. Bullies turned the demonstration into a riot, offending women around the country. The constitutional amendment became a live issue again. Miss Paul's organization, later known as the Woman's Party, kept agitating for the amendment, forcing the more conservative National American Woman Suffrage Association to increase its efforts too. In 1915 the NAWSA took a great step forward by making Carrie Chapman Catt its president. Mrs. Catt had briefly been its president earlier, then for years was head of the International Woman Suffrage Alliance, and finally had been leader of the campaign to secure woman suffrage in New York by a state referendum. There she created the largest grass roots movement for equal suffrage ever seen, and though defeated in the 1915 election, her group had such momentum that it was expected to prevail next time around, as it did.

As president once more of NAWSA, Mrs. Catt performed the same feat on a national scale. State units were revitalized. An efficient national staff was assembled. When New York State went for suffrage in 1917 it was clear that votes for women was an idea whose time had come. No one could say any longer that women did not desire it. Nor could they say that men would not accept it. At this point the Woman's Party became a liability. It employed the English strategy of blaming the party in power and campaigning against it at the polls. This had a certain logic in England, where the ruling party did actually have the power to enfranchise women. It made little sense in America, where neither party had the strength in Congress to do so and both were divided on the issue. Only a nonpartisan coalition would give women the vote.

Even worse, the WP refused after America entered the war to abandon its attack on President Wilson, though he had now become the symbol of American patriotism and national destiny. It went on picketing the White House and condemning "Kaiser Wilson" for waging war on behalf of democracy abroad while refusing to advance it at home. Mrs. Catt knew that Wilson and other liberal politicians were eager to embrace woman suffrage if a face-saving means of doing so were offered. The WP made it hard for them because to change position in the face of its actions would imply that politicians had given way under pressure, rather than surrendering to the demands of conscience. As this was in fact the case, politicians were all the more eager to seem uncoerced. War work proved to be the way out of this impasse. Women volunteered in large numbers as bond salespersons, bandage rollers, and the like, and participated more directly by taking jobs in industry left vacant when workers became servicemen. This enabled Wilson to say that women had earned the right to equal citizenship and removed all doubts as to their political fitness.

Wilson would probably have come out for woman suffrage sooner than he did had the WP stopped picketing him. Party members refused to give up, even when arrested and force-fed. The NAWSA did the only thing possible. It condemned the WP despite the government's tactics (which were so odious that they had to be abandoned anyway). Wilson could then claim that the WP represented only a handful of cranks, while the great majority of suffragists had shown themselves to be patriotic and responsible. In 1918 Congress passed the Nineteenth Amendment, and after more than a year of hard lobbying it was ratified just in time for women to vote in the 1920 election. A majority of those who did went for Harding. This was perhaps unfair to Wilson, but he was not a candidate for reelection and, in any case, many fewer congressional Democrats than Republicans had supported the Nineteenth Amendment.

The outcome of this great crusade was less glorious than expected. The argument that women would put through needed reforms when enfranchised was proven false. It soon became clear that there was no "woman vote." Women voted much as men did, except on moral issues like prohibition and the sexual habits of politicians. Women were rather more responsive to the peace issue. Even so, Jane Addams noted glumly later that congresswomen were united only by their common enthusiasm for a larger army and navy. Some felt that women actually had more power without the vote than with it. When they did not vote their influence was incalculable. When they did vote it could be measured and was found not to make much difference one way or another. The leaders of organized womanhood could no longer purport to represent a vast constituency. In consequence, while they had been moderately successful in promoting reforms before the vote, they got almost nothing they asked for in the 1920s. This was partly a function of the political climate. Reforms of every sort languished in the 1920s. Feminist leaders did not find this thought consoling. Mrs. Catt formed the League of Women Voters to succeed the NAWSA which, its object having been secured, went out of business. The LWV was very small compared with the NAWSA. The Women's Trade Union League and the Consumers' League declined. The General Federation of Woman's Clubs turned its attention to dirty movies and home appliances. For decades men had spoken in worried tones of the woman movement. Now it was no more.

The failure of feminism was prefigured by its success. Feminists were concerned with everything that affected the condition of women—jobs, education, domestic life. But most women did not object to the feminine condition as such. Working women were narrowly concerned with on-the-job issues that feminism was ill equipped to deal with. Middle-class women objected to specific abuses, few of which affected them directly. Social feminism was only marginally occupied with the woman question. The woman movement flourished by subordinating all else to equal suffrage, a cause most middle-class women could agree on once it was established that by voting they would promote reforms. To win the vote feminists played down their other goals. When they got it, feminists were deprived of the one issue that had broad appeal. Worse still, when the vote failed to bring the promised benefits, feminism was discredited.

The Progressive era was the greatest age in history for American women. Yet they did not get what they most wanted, the abolition of child labor, and what they did get, woman suffrage, had disappointing consequences. This seems not to have bothered many middle-class women, probably because they were a satisfied group. Their activity in the Progressive era flowed not so much from oppression as from their relative lack of it. Because they were stronger, and the old barriers weaker, insulting limitations on them were removed. When this was done most women lost interest in reform. But militant feminists had cause for despair precisely because they had won such a great victory, and, accordingly, had entertained high hopes for what could be built on it.

Their final reward was to see a new generation of young women emerge in the 1920s who were not politicized at all in feminist terms. They took what had been won for granted and concentrated on their own needs and pleasures. Feminists argued that the new generation, though happier, was not much better off than the last. Women were still discriminated against. Their marital and domestic situations were as difficult as before. No one listened, nor would again for almost fifty years. The generation of women that won the vote was the most brilliant and accomplished ever. It produced not only great feminists like Carrie Chapman Catt, but great social reformers like Jane Addams, Florence Kelley, and many others. Yet for feminists all this success was bought at a fatally high price. Their greatest generation left no heirs.

Most gains for women in those years were accidental, even when desired. Victorian women had worn confining, sometimes dangerous clothes. They often died in childbirth, and if not, frequently had more children than they wanted. Physicians did them more harm than good, partly through ignorance, also because radical gynecological surgery was thought to help personality disorders. A woman bothered by unwanted sexual desires might, for example, have her clitoris removed—a barbarism proscribed in England but practiced here until the twentieth century. Fashion and medicine alike conspired in the nineteenth century to make women's hard lot even more so.

In the twentieth century matters improved considerably. Feminists had tried in vain earlier to reform women's dress. By 1915 or so it was clear that women meant to dress more sanely. Skirts got shorter. The slip replaced layers of petticoats. The corset gave way to a simple elastic girdle. Drawers were replaced by panties. This transformation, which began in the Progressive era, was in practical terms worth considerably more to women than the vote. It was a physical emancipation that no one planned, but which liberated women all the same. Some feminists were afraid that bare arms and legs might be too sexy. But though revealing, the new fashions were not more erotic than older ones with their exaggerated bosoms and compressed waistlines. Once men adjusted to the shock of seeing rather more of women than before, their heartbeats returned to normal. Lust seems not to have increased much, if at all.

Fashion and custom changed together. Where once women could only play croquet and perhaps a decorous game of lawn tennis, all but the violent contact sports became open to them—bicycling and horseback riding astride, swimming, golf, even mountain climbing. Motorcars were easier to drive than a team of horses. This too was liberating. On the other hand, the much-praised improvement of domestic appliances did not benefit middle-class women greatly. They had not previously done their own housework anyway, and in time losing servants would cancel out the advantages of electric kitchens to a degree. Nor did the improvement of appliances do working-class women a lot of good at first, being still too costly. Women of all classes were greatly helped by advances in medical science. Conception became better understood and by the end of the era contraception was too, at least among middle- and upper-class women. Radical gynecological surgery declined, perhaps because psychoanalysis now seemed a more appropriate cure for personality and behavioral disorders. Feminists would complain, rightly in many instances, that psychoanalysis was only a more subtle way of keeping women in their place. It glorified maternity, submission, domesticity, and other "womanly" traits. But it was, at least, a considerable advance over radical surgery. Once the risks of maternity were reduced women began to outlive men. This had little effect on custom. Men went on marrying women younger than themselves.

There is some irony in the fact that what helped women most in the Progressive era were the things no one planned. Feminists did not get much of what they wanted, and much of what they did get had mixed effects. The condition of women improved anyhow. They did not then, nor would they later, achieve functional equality with men. But they were freed from clothing, customs, and medical practices that had done much harm. Sexual liberation of a sort was not far off. Even without it women in the Progressive era lived freer lives than before. Physical, and to a degree, social freedom were no substitute for economic and legal equality, feminists insisted. They were wonderful things to have all the same. They did not come wholly by accident. Feminist propaganda, even feminist example, helped by making women out to be stronger, brighter, more independent than old stereotypes allowed. But the growth of affluence, leisure, education, and the increased emphasis on consumption as against production helped too, as did the general liberalizing of taste and custom that marked the era. These foreshadowed and promoted the greater changes to come. Many progressive reforms were disappointing. But the improvement of everyday life made most Americans, women especially, better off than they had ever been.

PROHIBITION

Prohibition ended up as the most unpopular of contemporary reforms. At the time there was no reason to suppose this would happen. Later, prohibitionists would be remembered as ax-wielding harridans, juiceless, joyless busybodies, and praying women. But among middle-class people in the Progressive era no cause was more respectable or ardently fought for. At first temperance was unpopular. But in the 1890s science began to prove that alcohol was a dangerous drug. Laboratory work established that liquor was a depressant, not a stimulant as was previously believed. Even in small amounts it depressed brain, heart, and muscular activity. In larger amounts it caused damage to the brain, heart, liver, and other organs. It lowered resistance to disease and harmed recovery. A study of idiocy and imbecility in the United States attributed 5 percent of all cases to parental drinking; 20 percent of a sample of 160,000 epileptics, it was said, owed their affliction to parental intemperance. Studies by life insurance companies showed that 7.7 percent of adult deaths in 1908 were caused by liquor. Reformers knew that liquor was associated with crime, vice, pauperism, and other evils. Liquor and machine politics were closely related. All phases of the industry were involved in politics because of taxes, licensing laws, and the saloon's role as political clubhouse. Brewers and liquor interests had powerful lobbies that corrupted politicians and newspapers. They worked to defeat woman suffrage, thinking rightly that women would vote for prohibition. These facts were heavily publicized. Thus, it was not only social workers who saw the cost of drinking close up, but ordinary middle-class people also became aware of the social, moral, economic, and political costs of the liquor traffic.

In 1895 the Anti-Saloon League was formed to coordinate the many local temperance societies. In 1908 it was operating in forty-three states. By 1915 it had a paid force of 1,500 people and perhaps another 50,000 volunteer speakers. While the Episcopal, Roman Catholic, and Lutheran churches remained aloof, other denominations gave it bases in communities all over the country. It gained its own publishing house in 1909, which soon was running three shifts and turning out 400 tons of literature a month. The league urged drys to vote only for candidates approved by the ASL. It also worked for better enforcement of existing laws. The ASL shredly focused on the saloon rather than on the entire liquor industry, and on production and distribution rather than consumption. Until 1913 it concentrated on local areas and only then, when half the counties in America had gone dry, did it go for a national amendment. The ASL did not attack personal consumption until 1917.

Though prohibition seemed to be a matter of the dry countryside against the wet cities it was more in the nature of a class struggle. Native-born middle-class people increasingly favored it, not only for its own sake but because it was thought that without alcohol the immigrant masses would be less troublesome. Some native-born working-class people and most working-class immigrants were against the prohibition amendment. Ratification of the amendment came about partly because of the war, which enabled prohibitionists to demand it as a war measure to conserve grain; partly because twenty-seven states were already dry by then, leaving only nine to be won over for the purpose of amending the Constitution. Given the ASL's enormous lobby, great resources, and the emergency these were not terribly hard to get, especially as the liquor interests had already been damaged by the War Prohibition Act. National prohibition differed from local prohibition mainly in that it proscribed the use as well as the production and distribution of alcohol. This was probably a mistake, though in practice, as with marijuana later, users were treated less severely than dealers for the most part.

When prohibition failed, its sponsors and their arguments were discredited. Yet the problem was a real one, among the most serious facing Americans, and remains so today. No doubt prohibition would have worked better had it been less complete. If wines and beer had been exempted the great criminal organizations, built mainly on bootleg beer, might not have flourished. Perhaps beer gardens on the European model would have replaced saloons. Still, it does seem that per capita alcoholic consumption has not risen in modern times to preprohibition levels. And modern beers, if more uniform and tasteless than before, are also less alcoholic. This is not much to show for the greatest experiment in liquor control undertaken by any major nation. Even so there is no reason for mocking those who attempted it. Prohibition was typically progressive in that it was based on scientific premises, advanced in an organized and efficient manner, shrouded in moral hyperbole, and expected to produce fantastic benefits. It had ambiguous consequences, which was also typical. The great flaw in prohibition was not that it was utopian, rather that it was class-based, a matter of the bourgeoisie addressing itself to the vices of the poor. In a sense this was what flawed the entire age of reform. Middle-class people were quick to judge the poor, and sometimes even the rich. They seldom looked as closely at themselves.

BIBLIOGRAPHICAL NOTES

A classic study is Daniel Bell, *Marxian Socialism in the United States* (1952). A thoughtful work which takes exception to the usual view that socialism peaked out in 1912 is James Weinstein, *The Decline of Socialism in America, 1912–1925* (1967). An excellent and unusually objective short history is John P. Diggins, *The American Left in the Twentieth Century* (1973). The best study of an anarchist leader is Richard Drinnon, *Rebel in Paradise: A Biography of Emma Goldman* (1961). Melvyn Dubofsky, *We Shall Be All: A History of the Industrial Workers of the World* (1969), is excellent and detailed. There is no really good study of immigration as a whole, but John Higham, *Strangers in the Land* (1955), is very good on nativism. Roy Lubove, *The Professional Altruist: The Emergence of Social Work as a Career, 1880–1930* (1965), and Allen F. Davis, *Spearheads of Reform: The Social Settlements and the Progressive Movement, 1890–1914* (1967), are very useful. On housing reform see Roy Lubove, *The Progressives and the Slums* (1962). See also Robert H. Bremner,

From the Depths: The Discovery of Poverty in the United States (1956). The standard survey of black history is John Hope Franklin, *From Slavery to Freedom* (1962). On feminism in this period see Alileen S. Kraditor, *The Ideas of the Woman Suffrage Movement, 1890–1920* (1965), and William L. O'Neill, *Everyone Was Brave* (1969). Joseph R. Gusfield, *Symbolic Crusade* (1963), and Andrew Sinclair, *Era of Excess* (1962), are helpful on prohibition.

5

SOCIAL THOUGHT AND SOCIETY

One cannot speak of a "progressive mind," for progressives disagreed with each other on many points. Yet the era had its own distinctive ideas, some of which were bitterly contested. Individualism had been the central doctrine of late nineteenth-century Americans. They believed in free will, that man made his own destiny. They also believed competition was the engine of progress. Society bettered itself through struggle. The weak failed and the strong prospered. This state of affairs was dictated by immutable laws of nature, though rules were necessary to insure that the struggle was fair. Otherwise, legislation could do nothing. Any tampering with natural laws would lead inevitably to ruin. Individualism was radical in severing the ancient connections that had bound humans together. People were not to help one another but only to drive others to the wall, lest they themselves be driven. It was also a conservative doctrine because it sanctified the status quo. All existing institutions, having survived, were obviously the fittest.

But whether radical or conservative, individualism was always brutal. If taken literally it would have precluded charity and nearly all public services. Few Americans went that far. Doctrine was tempered with common sense and sometimes mercy. But these views meant that poverty had to be seen as socially desirable, nature's way of keeping the unfit from multiplying, though in reality they did so at a far greater rate than middle-class people with their small families—an inconvenient fact that was always overlooked. And such views meant that there could be no reform, since by definition reform was retrogressive. To change artificially what had developed naturally would destroy the delicate mechanism by which God and nature conspired to uplift society. These ideas, contradictory and often untrue though they were, served important functions. They seemed to explain the growth of American wealth and power. They provided the comfortable with good reasons to neglect or exploit the poor. "God has intended the great to be great and the little to be little," said Henry Ward Beecher, the most successful preacher of his time. Of the poor Beecher remarked, "the man who cannot live on bread and water is not fit to live." Scholars, lawyers, and scientists pretty much agreed that what was, was good.

But it was not. The economy boomed and slumped repeatedly. In the name of individual rights and natural law, men were worked to death and businesses looted. Hundreds of firms perished because Standard Oil proved its fitness by getting more railroad rebates than did competitors. Order, security, brotherhood were all sacrificed for the sake of abstract and supposedly immutable doctrines benefiting the few at the expense of the many. Victorians equated wealth with virtue, yet plainly the rich were seldom virtuous, and the virtuous seldom rich. So arid and contradictory a view of life could never engage the best American minds even at its peak and actually invited the best minds to attack it.

THE REVOLT AGAINST FORMALISM

Many American intellectuals rejected the abstract, formalistic logic of laissez-faire, as Morton White has shown, and sought to explain life in more dynamic ways. They meant to understand social evolution, not merely to proclaim it. They were led by such men as the philosopher John Dewey, Supreme Court Justice Oliver Wendall Holmes, Jr., and the economist Thorstein Veblen. What made them important was not ends reached, but means used. They replaced logic, abstraction, and deduction with change, experience, and common sense. Against formalism they employed historicism and cultural organicism. Historicism explained facts by reference to earlier facts. One understood the Constitution, for example, not by analyzing the text but by studying the men who wrote it, the interests they meant to defend, the precedents they had in mind, and the experiences which had formed them. Cultural organicism, which saw all the parts of a social system as related, attacked the problems of one social science with material derived from others. Thus poverty would not be seen as a function of character, but as a consequence of certain psychological, sociological, economic, and even political forces. Holmes expressed the fundamentals of legal realism in language that could as easily have been used by innovators in other disciplines. "The life of the law has not been logic: it has been experience." The new social thought did not believe in natural laws that explained all behavior, but in constantly changing processes. Most critics of laissez-faire believed that these processes could be understood and manipulated so that progress could be willed rather than merely awaited. As much as anything, that belief is why we are justified in calling the generation in power after about 1900 "progressive." Victorians believed in social progress also, but passively. Progressives were activists. Through what John Dewey termed "creative intelligence" and others called "practical idealism" they would build the kind of society that before them people had only dreamed of.

The antiformalists seem now often to have been mistaken on specific points. But even when wrong their conclusions seem to have been arrived at rightly. They preferred evidence to logic, experience to abstract principle. They saw life as infinitely various and mutable. What was daring in their time soon became commonplace. Yet their points of view are still governing assumptions in history and the social sciences. Although the idea of inevitable progress as such was discredited long ago, we are nearly all progressives still in the sense that we use the same methods, believe in reform, and see the human condition much as they did—a sign, perhaps, of their power, or our lack of it.

The strength of progressive social thought was also its weakness.

Individualists believed nothing could be done about inequities. All one could hope for was that in due time evolution would erase them. Most progressive thinkers took the opposite line, saying that evolution could be controlled and accelerated to bring about social justice, perhaps in their lifetime. But time would show that the more disinterested a reform, the harder it was to get. Middle-class people did well for themselves, organizing effectively on their own behalf, supporting pure food and other legislation that helped them directly as consumers. Businessmen got more efficient government and special bills like the Federal Reserve Act, which were of great value to them. It was very hard to get better housing, higher wages, or to abolish child labor and other evils. Even when legislation was passed it was frequently not enforced, or, as in the case of child labor, it was overturned by the courts. Sometimes reforms were poorly thought out. Other times they could not be translated into reality. Breaking the chains inhibiting social thought, as the antiformalists did, was one thing; providing workable new ideas was quite another.

The problem of community was a case in point. Nothing troubled progressive intellectuals more than the loss of it. Americans had complained of baleful cities even before there were any here. For much of the nineteenth century people continued to live in small towns and rural areas, making fears of the city academic. By 1900, however, the balance of population was so clearly tipping in favor of urban areas as to cause widespread alarm. The difficulty was not just that cities were iniquitous, full of sin and merriment, but even more that they drove people apart. Towns were egalitarian, intimate, neighborly, In them people governed themselves and took care of one another. People in cities were mobile, anonymous, and governed by odious machines. This encouraged "selfish individualism," an attitude which progressives thought responsible for crime, immorality, divorce, socialism, and everything else they disliked.

The problem was how to build a new sense of community in the urban context. To most progressives socialism was out of the question. Social settlements, which were supposed to inspire communality, did not—at least not on the necessary scale. Many hoped the new communications technology would help, as perhaps it did. The mass media were building a kind of mechanical folk culture. Yet progressives felt these new forms of communication transmitted the wrong values. Movies were no substitute for town meetings, they insisted. Most progressives held that schools were natural instruments for building up community life—one reason why they were so interested in education. Schools had their uses, but local school boards were invariably conservative and striking changes were therefore all but impossible. It was never clear anyway just what sort of change would be needed to revive community spirit.

A more sophisticated, though not necessarily more successful, idea concerning community was the argument for social control advanced by the sociologist E. A. Ross. The small Iowa town he grew up in exemplified community at its best, Ross believed. Having been raised on individualism he found much to admire in it too. But he appreciated that small towns were anachronisms and that social order was not compatible with unchecked individualism. If individuals had to be constrained, Ross wanted it done intelligently. The police power alone was not enough to build the good society. Ross argued for more subtle forms of coercion—public opinion, education, example, illusion, and especially "social religion." *Social Control* (1901) was an important book and the phrase itself became common currency in the Progressive era. But social control was not a blueprint, and it did not solve the problem of reconciling social needs with private rights. Ross and most progressive intellectuals disagreed with the great philosopher Josiah Royce, who said "it is the State, the Social Order, that is divine. We are all but dust, save as this Social Order gives us life." They thought the individual more important than that. Yet for society's sake—and that is to say for his own too—he had to be disciplined. Repression was impossible in a free society, and most progressives never considered it. But was not the humane manipulation Ross envisioned dubious also? How much of it could a free people take and still remain free? Social control, for all its popularity, raised as many questions as it answered.

The best minds of the age struggled with the problem of community. That they failed to solve it was not discreditable. Later generations would fail too. But it was characteristic of progressive intellectuals that in attempts to solve it they wound up embracing what they were against. Although they disliked bigness, centralization, and bureaucracy, they themselves wanted to regulate business and promote communal values. In doing so they preferred paternalism to unionization. Democratic only in theory, they favored decision making by experts, what one sociologist called "societal engineering" and another, the "scientific management of mankind." The result was that progressives moved further toward a public order that was centralized, bureaucratic, and esoteric—in the sense that decisions were made in obscure and complex ways that ordinary citizens could not judge properly.

EFFICIENCY

Few words were more widely used in the Progressive era than "efficiency." But what efficiency meant was not always clear. The word was applied to at least four different concepts, according to Samuel Haber: personal effectiveness; the energy input-output of a machine; the input-output ratio of dollars in business; and social harmony with government by a competitively selected elite. Frederick W. Taylor, the father of scientific management, used the word in all four ways. Taylor started as a patternmaker, became a machinist, then chief engineer of the Midvale Steel Company. Later he worked as an independent consultant, but his basic ideas were formed at Midvale—not only his schemes to put industrial planning and management on a scientific basis, but his moral values as well. These were typical of his time, emphasizing the character-building effect of hard work and praising the strenuous life of workshop and foundry. "The Midvale Steel Company," says Haber, "was to Taylor what the Big Horn Mountains were to Theodore Roosevelt."

Taylor at first thought the merits of scientific management were so obvious that industry would rush to adopt it. But by 1910 he concluded that too many businessmen were backward and too many industries noncompetitive for his ideas to flourish unaided, so he began cultivating public opinion. This meant that his ideas had to be softened. Scientific management was a hard, elitist system according to which engineers worked out the one best way of doing a thing and then ordered workers to comply with it. To make the system more attractive Taylor insisted that the "whole people" stood to gain from efficiency. This was a doubtful but attractive point. In 1910–11 it was widely seized on, thanks especially to Louis D. Brandeis's argument in the Eastern Rate Case.

This important case involved a number of railroads that were seeking rate increases. Brandeis represented shipping interests and maintained that the railroads' problem was not low income but excessive costs resulting from bad management. He argued that if they introduced scientific principles of management they would save a million dollars a day and have no need of rate increases. As described by Brandeis scientific management had enormous appeal. Most progressives disliked conflict and were grateful for ways of getting what they wanted without it. Scientific management seemed to them an ideal solution to the whole problem of industrial strife. If great savings were effected industry could cut prices and raise wages. Everyone would benefit and the social struggle would be at an end.

Brandeis seems to have believed this himself. In his view, cost cutting, together with other efficient practices such as price fixing and fair trade laws, would do the job. Though he was against certain business techniques, and thus was anathema to most capitalists, this progressive lawyer and future Supreme Court justice believed in the business system. Brandeis felt that as managers improved their products, reduced waste, and cooperated with each other intelligently, "the great industrial and social problems expressed in the present social unrest will one by one find solution." Though not many were quite so optimistic as he was, a great surge of interest in efficiency followed the Eastern Rate Case, lasting for about five years. It seemed as if a shortcut to the good society had been found that all decent people could agree on.

These happy prospects were soon blighted. Industries did not rush to avail themselves of scientific management. Some reformers thought it was dehumanizing. They attacked it for dividing jobs up into excessively small or boring segments, for turning men into machines, as indeed Taylor wanted to do. Socialists had mixed feelings. On the one hand, Taylorism was a sophisticated form of exploitation; on the other, a step toward the scientifically planned economy. It was hard to decide which view a Socialist should take. Organized labor provided the most effective resistance. Unionists never believed that cost cutting would raise wages. They resented being manipulated and were against the downgrading of skills Taylorism involved; they also resented the implicit charge that scientific management was needed because workers loafed on the job. They kept scientific management out of government manufacturing arsenals.

Taylorism was important not so much for what it accomplished as for what it revealed. Progressives like Walter Lippmann and Louis Brandeis were attracted to scientific management because they thought it would help business professionalize itself, which in turn was supposed to make businessmen more socially responsible. Scientific management was also desirable because it did not require appeals to conscience, which progressives had little faith in over the long run. By placing its trust in engineers, scientific management met the progressive requirement that things be run by nonpartisan experts. The only trouble was that it did not work. Cutting costs was not too difficult, but otherwise it was impossible to achieve the larger social objectives that had originally made Taylorism attractive to liberal intellectuals. There was no way, for instance, to make companies return part of their savings to workers in the form of wages. Professionalization did not automatically improve character. Efficiency by itself meant little; what counted was the environment in which it was achieved. To realize the promise of social engineering in this sense meant first to change the social order. As the function of reform was not to change society but to save it, the larger promise of social engineering could not possibly be realized.

HIGHER EDUCATION

Even before World War I universities demonstrated what other progressive ideas meant in practice. American universities were committed to research, practical service, and, sometimes, liberal culture. In the Progressive era they were also supposed to advance democracy. The University of Wisconsin was said by Lincoln Steffens to perform these duties best. The boundaries of the university are the boundaries of the state, it was declared; and Wisconsin did indeed perform services for business, agriculture, and government, while offering instruction in a growing list of practical subjects from animal husbandry to journalism. More and more state universities followed Wisconsin's example. But in fact, though individual professors had a great effect on reformers, universities, even Wisconsin, were undemocratic. Faculties lacked power, and usually tenure. Presidents grew stronger. Universities became more like one another. Accrediting, a great force for uniformity, started in 1913. Thirteen years earlier the Association of American Universities had begun harmonizing and perhaps raising standards of graduate instruction. Imitation was one reason for similarity, rivalry another. Where one institution led, others had to follow if they wished to remain competitive. Common problems were another reason for uniformity, also for bureaucratization.

As universities expanded they also became, in varying degrees, more representative of the whole nation. Students and faculty alike came from a greater range of socioeconomic, religious, and ethnic backgrounds—a result of the upward mobility that was enlarging the middle class as a whole. Professional schools and departments competed with each other for money and prestige, not just locally but frequently on a national scale. Internal diversity made bureaucratic norms a low but tolerable common denominator holding the university together. Universities became more businesslike. Where once the aim was merely to encourage mental discipline, universities now meant to prepare students for careers. Schools of business proliferated. Boards of trustees, formerly composed of ministers, now drew heavily on the business community. Economist Thorstein Veblen feared universities were becoming just another arm of business long before the 1964 Berkeley Free Speech movement made that charge fashionable. Though overdrawn, this picture was not entirely false. In a business civilization most universities would have to pay their way by one means or another. Perhaps the surprising thing was that universities still managed to support research; teach philosophy, among other impractical subjects; and sometimes nourish the arts. A few even hired Veblen, though he was unpopular with students and faculty alike and—to the extent they understood him—loathed by businessmen.

When universities in the Progressive era were applauded, it was for being democratic, egalitarian, progressive, and sometimes efficient. When they were criticized it was frequently because they were said to be custodians of an obsolete culture and bastions of privilege. This was mostly nonsense. Nearly all university students were middle class. Only a few elite institutions and fraternites played at being aristocratic. But universities were far from egalitarian precisely because they were middle class. They tried to be efficient and practical, hence progressive. Yet they were careful about social reforms, and discouraged students and faculty from promoting them. Custodians of traditional culture were not all that common and were on the defense anyway—both because the spirit of the age was hostile to cultural pretension and, even more, because new developments in art and literature were making what they taught old-fashioned. The central feature of American universities, whatever was said of them, was that they were becoming more uniform, centralized, bureaucratic, and big, like America itself.

CHANGING STANDARDS OF CULTURE AND MORALITY

When the era began there was little reason to suppose that culture and morality would not go on as before. After much struggle, the Victorians had established the primacy of moral values. Morality was the touchstone of all things American, but especially of literature, which had a special mission to uplift and instruct. Much of what the world judged great was deficient by these standards. Theodore Roosevelt, whose taste was better and more catholic than most of his peers, thought Chaucer was "needlessly filthy." Earnestness was more important than genius, thus TR preferred Robert Grant to Tolstoy and Edgar Fawcett to Hamlin Garland. History was seen as the transmission of Protestant ideals and Anglo-Saxon culture. Most people who thought about it agreed with TR that "the greatest historian should also be a great moralist." Literature meant chiefly English literature, though Emerson and Whittier were much admired. Melville was ignored. Whitman still made people uneasy. The great publishing houses, quality magazines, and Eastern universities provided traditional literature with solid institutional bases.

As late as 1912, when President Taft came to New York to help celebrate the birthday of William Dean Howells, grand old man of national letters, it seemed that taste and morality were still as they had been. Yet in a few more years the old order was all but shaken down by new people and new ideas. Its custodians imagined culture to be rational and knew it was disciplined. This was precisely what was wrong with it, romantic insurgents declared loudly after 1910. Inspired from abroad by Sigmund Freud, H. G. Wells, Henri Bergson, among others, they proclaimed the virtues of spontaneity, intuition, and sensuality. People like Van Wyck Brooks, John Dos Passos, Randolph Bourne, Floyd Dell, and many more scorned academic painting, preferring first the naturalistic ashcan school of Robert Henri and the Eight, then after the Armory Show of 1913, cubism, expressionism, and other avant-garde schools. In poetry Longfellow gave way to Ezra Pound and Amy Lowell. An unprecedented cultural flood burst the banks of Victorian taste and established the primacy of the new in art and culture. The convention that art was to promote established moral principles collapsed, seemingly overnight. To some, art was now its own reason for being. To others it was a means of changing the world, or at least American sensibilities. Still others, notably the ashcan artists, used it to advance socialism. Whatever its uses, the new art utterly destroyed the genteel cultural tradition, as Henry F. May has shown.

In the nineteenth century all great art seemed accessible to ordinary people. If inexpert they could not appreciate music, poetry, and painting as much as the more highly cultivated did, but they could enjoy and profit from art all the same. Modern art required more open-mindedness, commitment, and frequently greater expertise as well. Much new art was too difficult for most people to follow. And the new literature, though easy to read for the most part, was morally offensive to many. The "innocent rebellion," as Henry May calls the first stage of modernism, did not last long; perhaps it ended as early as 1917. But in that short time America moved culturally from the nineteenth to the twentieth century. Art thereafter was "modern," hence closed to great numbers of middle-class people, some of whom now came to depend on popular culture for the moral guidance high culture used to provide them with.

This was not what rebellious innovators had in mind. The socially conscious among them had hoped to democratize culture. This was the aim of Van Wyck Brooks, then a young critic, who helped rediscover American literature, rescuing it from the academy and in particular elevating Walt Whitman to first place among American writers. "Whitman—how else can I express it—precipitated the American character," Brooks wrote. Whitman was valuable not only because his poetry was spontaneous, intuitive, and the like, but also because he was a poet of the people. Elsewhere in his important book *America's Coming-of-Age* (1915), Brooks argued that a crucial discovery just made was that the lower social and cultural orders "have a certain humanity, flexibility, tangibility which are indispensable in any programme: that Tammany has quite as much to teach Good Government as Good Government has to teach Tammany, that slang has quite as much in store for so called culture as culture has for slang. . . . "

While traditional culture celebrated Anglo-Saxon values, insurgents looked elsewhere, often among the poor and foreign. One critic made a serious joke when he said that Howells should be admired because he had managed to write well even though a WASP. "What if Howells be a native American of Anglo-Saxon origin? Homer was blind. Coleridge was a slave to opium. Poe drank." No one put the alien case better than Randolph Bourne, who though poor and crippled from birth graduated from Columbia to become one of the country's best young critics during the few years before his death in 1918 at the age of 32. Bourne argued that the melting-pot idea showed a colonial mentality, for according to that idea, rather than making something new America was to go on pressing immigrants into an obsolete Anglo-Saxon mold. Bourne called instead for a "trans-national America" where diverse heritages would flower. Had the Jews and the Germans melted on arrival, how much less interesting would New York and Wisconsin be, he pointed out. If America was not simply to be England writ large, it would have to cherish what it now disdained—foreign peoples and their alien ideas.

Bourne overstated the danger. Immigration had already guaranteed that America would not be another Britain. Cultural insurgents were destroying Anglo-Saxon primacy and importing alien notions as fast as they could. But he rightly feared that Americans would go on disliking ethnicity where it made for differences on serious things like art and politics. Immigrants would retain their religion, their prejudices, sometimes their taste in foods. Much of the rest would be lost. The higher patriotism Bourne hoped would frame a national consciousness based on different heritages did not emerge. The country was held together instead by old-fashioned nationalism, standardized commodities, and popular culture—an outcome that dismayed custodians of the traditional culture and new insurgents alike.

In the twentieth century the old moral principles became hard to sustain, both in theory and practice. Where morality was once viewed as absolute it now became relative. Instrumentalism, the most powerful modern philosophy, had some effect here because it was concerned not so much with what was right as with what worked. Victorians were supposed to search their consciences and then do the right thing. Instrumentalists were expected to decide first what needed to be done and then figure out some morally acceptable way of doing it. If it really was necessary, an acceptable way of accomplishing it was always to be found, providing one was not too squeamish. A great many things that had once been black and white were now colored gray. The most striking example of how this worked was provided by John Dewey after American entry into the world war.

To younger American intellectuals especially, Dewey's had seemed the ideal philosophy for a growing country in need of reform. It was, they thought, both moral and flexible, a nice change from the stiff and fussy ethics of old. Before 1914 Dewey had seemed to favor peace. But in 1915 he published *German Philosophy and Politics* in which he made a significant distinction between force and violence. Force was morally neutral, therefore an act could not be condemned merely because it employed force. A man could support war, accordingly, if he proved that it was neither wasteful nor unintelligent. This would make it nonviolent, Dewey appeared to say. "The criterion of value," he wrote, "lies in relative efficiency and economy of the expenditure of force as a means to an end." If that meant anything it was that force, however odious, was fine so long as used efficiently in a good cause.

Dewey's admirers did not grasp this meaning until America entered World War I and Dewey began writing articles explaining why it was the pragmatic thing to do. His book *Creative Intelligence* (1917) had just come out, and Dewey drew on it to show "innocent" and "naive" young pacifists where they erred. Their conscience was attached to forces moving in a hopeless direction. The answer was "to connect conscience with the forces that are moving in another direction. Then will conscience itself have compulsive power. . . . " This was almost to say that might makes right. Bourne, who would soon write bitterly that "war is the health of the state," rejected his old teacher's arguments. War, he pointed out, is an absolute condition, having no other end but itself. "Peace comes through victory or exhaustion, and not through creative intelligence." Bourne did not live to see it, but the peace treaty would make his point clearer. He knew anyway that Dewey's lame effort to make moral sentiment and blind force compatible showed that instrumentalism was useless when most needed.

In his finest essay on Dewey, "Twilight of Idols," Bourne wrote that instrumentalism, which he called "scientific method applied to 'uplift'," worked "when we were trying to get that material foundation for American life in which more impassioned living could flourish. . . . " But he continued, it "no longer works when we are faced with the inexorable disaster and the hysterias of the mob." It had produced a generation of young people with "no clear philosophy of life except that of intelligent service, the admirable adaption of means to ends. They are vague as to what sort of society they want, or what kind of society America needs, but they are equipped with the administrative attitudes and talents necessary to attain it." Bourne may have been unfair in saying that Dewey had led a whole generation to subordinate values to technique. It was, after all, a very American habit. Bourne was surely right to say that a philosophy which embraced what intelligence could not control was hardly worth having.

Dewey was only one of many intellectuals who took the same line. What they showed was the weakness of progressive thought as a whole. Progressive intellectuals generally agreed with Dewey that society was plastic, change inevitable, and creative intelligence the way to guide it. Yet most accepted a war that stood for everything they were supposedly against—blind force, destruction, submission to the flow of events. Wilson brought them around by the simple act of saying, all appearances to the contrary, that World War I would become liberal, democratic, and progressive if the Allies won. Intellectuals bought this because they wanted to believe it and because their philosophy enabled them to. Yet for want of anything better most American intellectuals are still instrumentalists of a sort. Those who pride themselves on being tough-minded carry even farther the doctrines that made entry into the first war so easy. They still confuse means and ends and go on thinking that by main force they can make history turn out as they would like. This is one of the chief legacies progressivism has bequeathed to us. Instrumentalism is like an old cloak that grows shabbier with use, but to which each new generation clings more tightly all the same.

Most Americans were little concerned with the moral questions raised by instrumentalism. They were, however, very much aware of changes in personal morality, especially as they affected sex. Victorians had possessed an extraordinary moral confidence, which was all the stronger for having been won so hard. The great challenge of evolution had been met by interpreting the scriptures poetically, thus solving the problem of how to square Genesis with Darwin and Lamarck. God was seen as the author of evolution and therefore of progress. It was discovered that He was also a social critic, a useful conclusion that put religion at the service of reform. These were successful devices. They reassured people that Christian virtues were still the best. But, while allowing for social change, the Victorians generally reinforced conventional morals. They felt standards of behavior to be so absolute that it was better to break than bend them. Thus, both men and women were called upon to be chaste. Since this was an impossible demand, prostitution flourished almost everywhere and was everywhere forbidden. It could not be legalized because that was to accept unchastity. It could not be dispensed with because lust would then have no safe outlets. So Victorians upheld chastity in theory while frequently turning a blind eye to its numerous violations in practice.

Divorce posed another kind of problem. All Victorians having agreed that marriage was the bedrock upon which civilization rested, divorces were consequently intolerable. But the divorce rate kept going up anyway. Liberal Christians met this problem by arguing, among other things, that divorce was good for marriage as an institution because it enabled bad marriages to be ended and good ones to be put in their stead. Most people resisted this argument all through the Progressive era, but in the end it prevailed. Since divorce could not be stopped it had to be redefined. This was not too difficult as reformers and conservatives both agreed on the primacy of marriage. To liberal Christians it was even possible to think of divorce as a way of putting marriage on a higher moral plane than before, when every kind of marital abuse had to be borne for civilization's sake.

Most Victorians regarded contraception as little better, if at all, than masturbation, which was horrible. Yet the birth rate declined rapidly. In 1850 the average family in Massachusetts had 5.6 persons in it. By 1900 one full member had been lost. Contraceptive devices were not readily available during the last half of the nineteenth century. In fact the law proscribed them nearly everywhere. This meant that abstinence was the principal means of avoiding conception. That the birth rate fell anyway suggested powerful motives were at work. Another reason for the birth rate's decline was that the average age of marriage was rising. In Massachusetts the average age of marriage for women in 1864 was 20.7 years. In 1901 it was 24.6, which meant that most women lost, in effect, four of their most fertile years. Another way of looking at it was to say that they reserved for personal use four more of the best years of their lives.

These facts upset moral conservatives, and frequently liberals as well. They appeared to signify a rise in license and self-indulgence. The resulting fears, however, were greatly exaggerated. To everyone's surprise civilization endured. It turned out that neither chastity, nor even perhaps monogamy, were essential to public order and civility. The divorce rate keeps rising still, yet marriage seems as popular as ever judging by the number of divorced people who remarry. While every step away from Victorian sexual standards continues to be denounced as another nail in society's coffin, society hangs together all the same, pornography and group sex notwithstanding. Where it does not, the causes are not sexual but have to do with poverty and other social problems. Knowledge of this would have given Victorians scant cheer. They were against sexual liberty not just because it was antisocial, but even more because it was wrong.

Moral conservatives had good reason to fear that smaller families and more frequent divorces were only the beginning. But they hurt their case by exaggerating events in their own time. More divorces, they said, meant the end of monogamy. Family limitation was "race suicide." The publication in the 1890s of so carefully written a book as Thomas Hardy's *Jude the Obscure* led one American critic to say that Hardy had trailed his talent in the dust, and another to charge that the book was "steeped in sex." Victorians were nearly always wrong in specifics, but generally right in thinking that each hesitant step away from prudery would lead to another. Since they also believed that in their time America had reached moral heights previously undreamed of it was hard for them to explain why sexual standards were falling.

Industry and ideology were mostly at fault for the changes in sexual standards, it now seems, though perhaps not equally. Industry made the city great, and the city made the family small. Large families were useful on the farm—and inexpensive, when farms were mostly self-sufficient. In the cities, where there was less room and everything cost more, children were a mixed blessing. Upwardly mobile families especially were aware of the relation between family size and standard of living. The result was a kind of iron law holding that the size of a family and its income are inversely related. This is true for second-generation Americans, whatever their religion, about as much as for the old stock. The falling birth rate showed that abstinence worked, but it did not work so well as prophylactics. The employment of women was another reason for the falling birth rate. There were two million working women in 1870, eight million in 1910. In the first decade of this century alone the proportion of women who worked rose from one-fifth to one-quarter of all adult females. Working women did marry and have children. But they had stronger motives than most for not wanting many.

Industry meant wealth, some of which trickled down; and wealth created the opportunity, perhaps also the desire, for pleasure. As the progressive economist Simon Patten observed, America was moving from a "pain or deficit" economy to a "pleasure or surplus" economy. When they were living in a developing nation, Americans had to work and suffer if a capital surplus was to be generated for reinvestment. But as the economy advanced, consumption became as important as production, perhaps more so. Instead of being urged to save, Americans were now asked to spend. They did not require much coaxing, the urge to live better being almost universal in modern times. All the same, it required a considerable change in attitudes since Victorians believed in self-denial for its own sake, especially when practiced by others.

The pleasure principle had been rising since the 1890s, at least. After 1900 the demand for recreational outlets became more insistent, and bowling alleys, dance halls, pool parlors sprang up to meet it. Professional sports, with baseball leading the way, grew rapidly. A couple of basic facts partly account for the new importance of recreation: first, real income was going up, so that often even rather poor families had money to spend on entertainment, if it was cheap enough; second, the work week was shrinking. Between 1900 and

1940 the average workweek declined from 56 to 41 hours, with most of this reduction having taken place by 1920.

No form of entertainment during the Progressive era was more vital than the moving picture, and movies had a great effect on public taste and morality. The first projector, Thomas Edison's Vitascope, went into commercial use in 1896. Early movies, mostly short and crude, were confined to arcades and vaudeville houses. In 1903 Edison made the first narrative film, *The Great Train Robbery*, and in 1905 the first house devoted exclusively to pictures opened in Pittsburgh. Since all that was needed was a room, projector, and chairs, thousands of "nickelodeons" sprang up around the country. Soon audiences were demanding better films, and growing revenues enabled producers to make them.

Films upset conventional moralists and custodians of culture for many reasons. On a larger scale than live entertainment they by-passed all existing channels of authority to make direct contact with the individual. This undermined church, school, and family, it was feared. Worse still, films were a purely recreational medium with little redeeming educational, religious, or social value. They were produced, it was thought in that anti-Semitic age, by unscrupulous money-crazed Jewish ex-garment manufacturers. Until 1912 or 1913 films were aimed mostly at working-class audiences. Some were comedies and Westerns. Many dealt with figures and themes familiar to the poor: policemen and burglars, factory workers, farmers, clerks, politicians, drunks, servants. These films were sentimental and melodramatic, yet not unrelated to real life. Middle-class people felt, though, that a mass medium devoted to such commonplace themes could only blight the national culture. Films were considered overstimulating, hence unhealthy, as well as sexually provocative. Besides the movies themselves, critics worried about the dark and potentially sinful theaters in which they were shown. Jane Addams called the nickelodeon "the house of dreams" and attacked it for contributing to juvenile delinquency, neurosis, sexual license, bad health, antisocial behavior, and even attempted murder. Another social worker called films a "new and curious disease," whose special victims were children from 10 to 14 years of age.

Middle-class people early demanded that, where movies were

concerned, the poor should be protected from themselves. However, though widely desired, censorship was hard to effect. For one thing, because producers were numerous and mobile censorship had to be imposed on the exhibitors. This was easier said than done since by 1912 there were at least 13,000 picture theaters. In time censorship became feasible. As films earned more money producers started making more elaborate and expensive ones, which attracted more affluent audiences. In 1914 the 3,000-seat Strand Theater opened in New York. It was the first large theater in the world devoted solely to motion pictures. Others soon followed so that while movie attendance went up, the number of theaters declined. Nickelodeons gave way in cities to great picture palaces, and in the neighborhoods, to medium-size theaters seating 600 to 1,000 people in some comfort. Films increasingly were geared to the middle-class audience and so were less offensive to censors. There were fewer theaters, making them easier to police. Finally, the hundreds of independent producers gave way to a handful of major studios, which were less difficult to coerce. Even so, it was not until the 1930's that censorship became fully effective.

Censors were able to do something about the content of films. What they could not touch was the general effect they had, even when clean and bourgeois. (And of course many were not. The first big sex film, *Traffic in Slaves*, nominally based on vice investigations, exploited sex in the name of morality—a technique later perfected by Cecil B. De Mille—and made the producer $45,000 in a few months on an investment of $5,700. In 1915 Theda Bara became the first movie sex symbol, thanks to her epic *A Fool There Was*.) The *Dial*, a literary magazine, said in 1914 that films showed "the demoralizing modern tendency to seek lines of least resistance in every form of activity, to convert education into amusement and work into play, without giving the least thought to the way in which the process softens the mental fibre and saps the character." Moralizing apart, this was exactly right. Movies were subversive of old ways, not chiefly because they were sexy, but because they provided instant gratification cheaply and on a massive scale.

The nineteenth century had been an age of work. The twentieth would be an age of play, not in the sense that people no longer needed to work, but in that they valued recreation more and labor less, and no longer believed as firmly in work for its own sake.

Employees came to feel that ample leisure should be a condition of employment. Movies were the sign of what was coming. They foreshadowed a revolution in values that would see the springing up of huge industries based on play, and later still the forming of a counterculture which rejected work so completely that it would constitute a new kind of leisure class, based not on wealth but on the freedom from it.

In the Progressive era Americans were already being encouraged toward self-indulgence, although somewhat hesitantly. It was advertising that provided the most direct encouragement. Cosmetics firms told women "how to Become Beautiful, Fascinating, Attractive." No one had to inquire why women needed to become more fascinating. Popular music was sometimes even more direct. "If you can't get your baby in the summertime, you won't get your baby at all," said one ragtime tune. Soon heated automobiles would greatly extend the mating season. The pleasure ethic included sexual pleasure, which was used to sell goods and was itself sold, inasmuch as movies and books got sexier. Necklines plunged, hemlines rose, inspiring the *New York Times* to announce editorially in 1914 that women's dresses had approached "the danger line of indecency about as closely as they could." In a few years the danger line had to be redrawn, as women seemed determined to expose more of themselves.

Affluence, leisure, and advertising made the pleasure ethic possible. But there was also an active propaganda furthering it, sometimes by accident. Although feminists were generally women of old-fashioned morals, all the same they urged women to be independent, self-sufficient, bold—in short, to be like men. Emancipated women found it hard to see why they should have the duties of men but not their pleasures. The double standard was undercut to a degree because women became less chaste. This was not the sort of freedom older feminists had in mind and many were discouraged by the fruit of their labors.

A more obvious propaganda was waged by self-conscious advocates of a new morality, such as Ellen Key, Havelock Ellis, H. G. Wells, Edward Carpenter, and others. All were foreigners; all were widely read in America; and all called, however vaguely, for different standards of sexual behavior. Miss Key, a Swedish writer and teacher, wanted women to have the right, as eventually they did in

Sweden, to bear children without getting married and without being penalized. Ellis, Wells, and Carpenter thought marriage was emotionally constraining. Ellis and Carpenter especially argued that people would be happier if less confined. These new moralists collectively had a broad, if not deep, influence during the Progressive era, as did some native sexual ideologists.

Political radicals sometimes called for an end to marriage on the ground that it made women a form of property. Most Socialists and most feminists did not follow this line—sometimes on principle, sometimes for fear that free love would crowd out the social solutions they meant to implement. But a notorious handful defied convention with mixed results. Max Eastman and Ida Ruah, who were both Socialists and feminists, solved the problem by getting married and then telling newsmen afterwards that they did not believe in it, but had gone ahead because not to would have been a nuisance. Many couples in Greenwich Village lived together proudly though unwed. The idea was to behave exactly as if married, which made the principle involved unclear to many. If a couple was wed in all but name, why not, as the Eastmans did, take the name and escape the bother? Some anarchists grasped the point. Feeling that monogamy was monogamy, whether recognized by the state or not, they rose above it. Free people mated freely, they argued, and tried to do so. Hutchins Hapgood, a journalist who knew some anarchists well and was himself a great womanizer, did not think their system worked at all. In theory anarchists were cleansed of bourgeois sentiments. But in truth they were products of the old order, however much they resented it. When someone they loved made love to another they felt jealous, a pain all the harder to bear because supposedly beneath them.

Birth control was the most tangible manifestation of changing sexual norms. Not many people turned to free love, but a great many wanted contraceptives, as the falling birth rate showed. The problem was how to get them. It was known that contraceptives existed. But law and custom alike proscribed them so fiercely that even many physicians were ill informed on the subject. Radical women were the first to attack this problem. Emma Goldman, the anarchist leader, studied contraception in Europe and tried to make it available to working-class women. She found much trouble and few allies. Margaret Sanger was more successful. As a visiting nurse in New York City she saw women die after trying to abort themselves. She was aghast at how little immigrant women knew about personal hygiene. In 1912 she wrote a series of articles for the Socialist newspaper *Call* dealing with venereal disease and related topics. The series had to be canceled when the Post Office Department denied the *Call* its mailing privileges.

As so often happens, repression had a radicalizing effect. Like Emma Goldman, Mrs. Sanger went to Europe and studied contraceptive techniques. She also wrote a pamphlet explaining them. Since this was illegal she could not distribute it in the United States. On her return in 1914 she instead began publishing a radical organ called the *Woman Rebel*, full of advice and revolutionary bombast. Though it did not say how to prevent conception, the *Woman Rebel* was loud enough to be indicted under the Comstock Act, which held that anyone using the mails to discuss unauthorized sex practices was dirty and should go to jail. Mrs. Sanger preferred to go abroad. But when her husband was arrested by Comstock, who had personally arranged to trick him into giving away a copy of her pamphlet, Margaret Sanger came back. The government finally decided not to prosecute her, though her husband was jailed. She was too, after opening an illegal birth control clinic in 1916.

Victorian morality won the battle while losing the war. Once it became widely known that effective contraceptives existed, Mrs. Sanger began getting help, mostly from middle- and upper-class women. This deradicalized her without defusing her. As rich women had different problems from poor women, the balance of Mrs. Sanger's argument shifted away from saving lives and toward promoting sexual freedom. In the past she had thought safety and pleasure equally good reasons for birth contol. But her new supporters particularly wanted to make love without fear. Birth contol advocates never stopped reminding people that poor women needed such help. Margaret Sanger made a point of telling women that sex was a great thing in its own right—if the woman was protected against unwanted pregnancies. Mrs. Sanger was not a new moralist or sexual radical in the sense of disdaining marriage. But by advocating sexual pleasure and assisting women to gain it she probably had more effect than any proponent of free love.

The pleasure ethic met heavy if ineffective resistance. All subsequent experience demonstrates that sexual freedom is hard to stop. While it can be slowed down by punishing offenders like Mrs. Sanger, this does little more than gain time. Conservatives fought thousands of delaying actions, the long-term effects of which seem to have been negligible. Orthodox morality enjoyed some successes, mainly when attacking prostitutes. Not much could be done about young people petting in bushes, still less in automobiles. Married people could not be made to have more children, though by banning contraceptives it could be made more difficult for them not to. The mass media would go on exploiting sex whatever restrictions were placed on them. This did not leave much but pornography and prostitution as objects of effective wrath. The postal authorities effectively contained pornography for years to come—though like all sinful pleasures it could never be wholly suppressed. So progressives turned to fighting commercial vice.

Ostensibly this was because prostitution was becoming more highly organized and ambitious. Rings of white slavers were thought to be drugging innocents on the city streets and whisking them off to bordellos in Mozambique. There is no reason to suppose that things were actually getting worse in the Progressive era. But there were vice investigations in many cities, conducted usually by citizens' groups such as the delightfully named Morals Efficiency Commission of Pittsburgh. Legal action normally followed, enabling antivice crusaders to publish reports with figures showing how many people were arrested, how many houses closed, how many fallen women, if any, saved. (In Pittsburgh none seem to have been uplifted, but Moral Efficiency Commissioners did go round telling the girls "to save money and think of their future.")

All this produced the customary illusion of success. Yet prostitution survived as always, and where it did not this had little to do with vice reform. Two things worked against prostitution. The first was that immigration ended with the coming of World War I. Many prostitutes serviced immigrants who lived alone because single or because their families were in the old country. After 1914 this supply of customers largely dried up. Second, as the changing moral climate allowed middle-class men to have relations more frequently with women of their own class, fewer resorted to prostitutes. Immigration and Victorian morality had made prostitution a big industry. With their passing it diminished, though this would not become clear until after World War I, since the army created a large but temporary demand. The apparent success of vice reform was a matter of luck. Having stumbled by accident on a failing vice, reformers congratulated themselves for curbing it. This delusion made it all the harder for them to deal with the real sexual changes going on, of which protitution's decline was only a symptom.

BIBLIOGRAPHICAL NOTES

Morton White, *Social Thought in America: The Revolt Against Formalism* (1957 ed.), is a searching work on five important progressive intellectuals. A fine study of the efficiency cult is Samuel Haber, *Efficiency and Uplift: Management in the Progressive Era, 1890–1920* (1964). An intriguing book, showing that most important progressives who were still active in the 1930s opposed the New Deal, is Otis L. Graham, Jr., *An Encore for Reform: The Old Progressives and the New Deal* (1967). An outstanding history of higher education in this period in Laurence R. Veysey, *The Emergence of the American University* (1965). Henry F. May, *The End of American Innocence* (1959), brilliantly deals with the transformation of American thought and culture during the years 1912–17. The exuberant vitality of young intellectuals is best captured in Van Wyck Brooks, *America's Coming of Age* (1915). Changing morals are discussed in William L. O'Neill, *Divorce in the Progressive Era* (1967). A rich and original interpretation of media power and social control is the unpublished dissertation by Garth S. Jowett, "The Motion Picture in America, 1894–1936" (University of Pennsylvania, 1972). James R. McGovern, "The American Woman's Pre-World War I Freedom in Manners and Morals," *Journal of American History* (September, 1968) is illuminating. The best book on its subject is David M. Kennedy, *Birth Control in America: The Career of Margaret Sanger* (1970). Two books that deal with the widespread anxiety about the decline of community are Jean B. Quandt, *From the Small Town to the Great Community* (1970), and R. Jackson Wilson, *In Quest of Community: Social Philosophy in the United States, 1860–1920* (1968).

6

WILSONIAN PROGRESSIVISM

Woodrow Wilson was an odd sort of man to become president. His father was a minister, and Wilson grew up to become, as one Catholic politician remarked, a Presbyterian priest. He was out of step with the times most of his life. In an age of scientific materialism he was religious, romantic, and impulsive. Wilson always wanted to be a great statesman, but disdained practical politics until very late in his life. Before 1910 it was doubtful he would ever rise high enough for statesmanship. Unlike Roosevelt, who climbed his way up the political ladder, Wilson became an academician. He did his graduate work at Johns Hopkins University, which had the best group of historians and social scientists in the country. They did not persuade Wilson to accept the realities of American political life. His doctoral thesis, published as *Congressional Government* in 1885, argued the superior merits of Britain's constitution. Wilson loved the British system because the prime minister, Wilson thought, was more powerful than the president of the United States and because in Parliament oratory counted whereas in Congress it did not. Critics liked his book precisely because it was steeped in irrelevant mugwump prejudices. Wilson went on in the next seventeen years to teach at Bryn Mawr and Princeton, and to write five books and a multivolume history of the United States, all of them commonplace and even reactionary. His denigration in them of the new immigrants would prove very embarrassing in 1912. Wilson was afraid of the trusts, but also of regulating them. Mostly he was a Jeffersonian and a gold Democrat who cared more for rhetoric than programs.

In 1902 Wilson became the president of Princeton University, where he displayed the same strengths and weaknesses he would exhibit as president of the United States. Wilson wanted to make Princeton into a university resembling Oxford, but with seminars as at Johns Hopkins. Princeton would then nurture not only the spirit, as when it was simply a church school, but the mind as well. The curriculum was revised, modern departments established, and preceptors added to supervise student reading, on the English model. In 1906 Wilson proposed to change both the physical setting and social life of Princeton. The snobbish eating clubs were to be abolished and students housed in quadrangles, each with its own dormitories, classrooms, and faculty. These changes were not intended to democratize undergraduate society, but to unify it. The clubs were anti-intellectual and divisive, the very opposite of that high-minded, intensely corporate life Wilson meant to establish. His plan was given to the faculty without warning and met stiff resistance. Some professors opposed his tactics, others his concepts, still others his whole administration. Wilson was overconfident and had not prepared the ground for his elaborate plan, enabling the alumni to save their eating clubs. This defeat reduced his power in the university, but gave him an undeserved national reputation as a champion of democratic and egalitarian principles.

Wilson finished himself at Princeton by fighting over the graduate school. Dean Andrew F. West wanted its new facilities built off-campus, as far removed from Wilson as possible. Wilson wanted in on-campus, where he could see that it was properly fitted into the university community. West won out because a friend of his died leaving millions to the graduate school, on the condition that it be built off-campus. This was too much money to refuse. Wilson accepted it and then resigned. His Princeton experience was typical of his public life. At first he was successful because conciliatory and persuasive. Then he lost touch, stiffened up, and refused to bargain. Every issue became a moral and personal one. In the end Wilson preferred defeat to compromise.

Despite his failure at Princeton Wilson was asked by George M. Harvey, a wealthy magazine publisher and gold Democrat, to run for governor of New Jersey in 1910. He was a happy choice from the Democratic machine's point of view, as it needed his moral stature to offset its own seamy record. Besides, James Smith, the Democratic boss, was assured that Wilson would play ball with him. The GOP was divided between progressive and old-guard factions, giving the Democrats a good chance to win. But Wilson almost muffed the election by talking about morality, the high cost of living, the tariff, and similar issues of little concern to New Jersey progressives. Then, all else having failed, Wilson was advised to exploit the growing sentiment for reform. He began attacking the trusts and promised to give the Public Service Commission power to fix utility rates. He would sponsor a corrupt practices bill. United States senators would be directly elected. And where he had been antilabor before, he now called for a workman's compensation act. Wilson climaxed this reversal by saying with a straight face, "I am and always have been an insurgent." Aided by the fact that railroad rates went up just before election day, Wilson won.

Since he believed deeply in any position he took, no matter how recently, Wilson put through nearly all the bills he had promised. And for good measure he added the initiative, referendum, and recall, plus a bill legalizing commission governments for municipalities. All this was done in one year, despite the opposition of Boss Smith, whom Wilson repudiated immediately on taking office, as he had to if his campaign pledges were to be redeemed. In 1912 Republicans won back control of the New Jersey legislature, putting an end to further reforms. This hardly mattered as his great success the year before had already made him a contender for the Democratic presidential nomination.

Most regular Democrats had little use for Wilson. Apart from stabbing Boss Smith in the back, as they thought, his manner was all wrong. "The time I met him, he said something to me, and I didn't know whether God or him was talking," a ward leader reported. The pros liked House Speaker Champ Clark on account of his regularity and backward ideas. William Jennings Bryan still had many friends and little affection for Wilson, who in 1907 had expressed the hope that some way would be found "to knock Mr. Bryan once and for all into a cocked hat." But Wilson had changed greatly since then, and Bryan inclined toward him, though not to the point of actual endorsement. Wilson's managers obtained the support of enough bosses to put him over at the nominating convention; though it took forty-six agonizing ballots to do so. He was by no means the first antimachine candidate to embrace the bosses when he had to, only the most pious.

Wilson tried to distinguish his program from Roosevelt's by calling it "the New Freedom." Ostensibly this meant that he stood for individualism, competition, and personal freedom. Many people thought so, and it may once have been true. But in 1912 there was little difference between the two candidates except as personalities. Wilson based his campaign on trust legislation, tariff reduction, and banking reform. Roosevelt, after being compelled to dilute the New Nationalism, differed with him on these points mostly in detail. Wilson favored nearly all the political devices progressives thought so important. While he did not go as far as Roosevelt on social justice issues, his mind was relatively open and within a few years he would embrace most of them. Wilson won, not because he offered a clear choice to the voters, but because the GOP was divided. Bryan campaigned hard for the ticket, and La Follette, who was still sore at Roosevelt, sat out the election. Wilson did not win by much, but his party gained control of both House and Senate anyway.

WILSON'S FOREIGN POLICY

Wilson's first important act as president, making Bryan secretary of state, said little about the kind of chief executive he would make. He owed his election to Bryan and so, in return, had to give him a big job. Today, when Bryan is only remembered as the narrow and foolish old man of the Scopes trial, his appointment as secretary of state seems peculiar. But at the time it made good sense. Nearly every living voter could remember the election of 1896 when Bryan, a little-known former congressman, had come out of nowhere to thrill the Democratic convention with his "Cross of Gold" speech, fuse the Populists and Democrats, and stump the country as no one had before.

After 1896 Bryan remained a great campaigner, but he showed himself to be no radical and not much of a politician. In 1899 he made the unbelievable mistake of persuading Democratic senators to vote for the peace treaty with Spain on the ground that America did not want the Philippines and would vote Democrats in to get rid of them. The election of 1900 was lost and Philippine independence also, neither of which Bryan desired. Bryan had other defects. He was for peace in peacetime and war in wartime. He substituted rhetoric for thought on every occasion. "One could drive a prairie schooner through any part of his argument and never scrape against a fact," David Houston, who served in Wilson's cabinet with him, once said. And Bryan dropped and added issues at will, so that the casual observer could never be sure at any given time what Bryan stood for. Yet he was a brave man, as he showed in 1896, and even more in 1915 when he resigned from the cabinet because of what he considered Wilson's dangerous stand concerning the sinking of the *Lusitania*—a courageous act, not diminished by its utter futility. Bryan endorsed virtually every reform there was. And he enjoyed the confidence of plain people, especially in the South and West, more than anyone else in his time. They knew he was provincial like themselves. These qualities made Bryan strong, while keeping him from being great.

All the same, Bryan was an adequate secretary of state, partly because Wilson was his own foreign minister. They agreed on nearly everything anyway until 1915. Both were moralists. Both were anticolonialists. Both were against war and for international trade, though Bryan went further than Wilson in wanting every Latin country to be in debt to Americans. Both believed it was the duty of America to raise up backward nations through good example. And both believed in arbitration treaties, which Bryan promoted feverishly. Bryan was criticized for not serving alcohol at official parties, but "grape juice diplomacy" went over well in the dry states. People complained of his habit of appointing deserving Democrats to diplomatic posts, however unqualified they might be. This made little difference because, while Wilson gave Bryan a free hand with the diplomatic corps, the president insisted that consular appointments, which were really important because they related to trade, be made on merit.

Wilson's foreign policy before the Great War was not much different from that of Taft or Roosevelt, except that it was more moralistic. The function of American diplomacy in those days had little to do with national security because that was not in danger. The purpose of foreign policy was chiefly to advance international trade and keep European powers out of the Western Hemisphere. To this end the country needed a big navy and aggressive economic programs overseas. Though Taft alone was known for "dollar diplomacy," he, Roosevelt, and Wilson all wanted more foreign trade and would go a long way to get it. Taft urged American bankers to invest abroad, especially in China. He also landed Marines in Nicaragua several times to restore stability and protect American investments.

When Wilson came into office it seemed that dollar diplomacy was finished because he withdrew American support for bank loans to China, which then were dropped. But time showed it was only that particular consortium he disliked. Wilson favored trade over investment abroad. Yet in 1917 he promoted a new consortium in China on terms he thought more favorable to Americans than the old. Wilson was always a faithful friend of exporters. He named Paul Reinsch, a longtime advocate of commercial expansion overseas, minister to China. His minister to Great Britain, Walter Hines Page, was also known to favor exports, as did William C. Redfield, Wilson's secretary of commerce. Redfield reorganized the Bureau of Foreign and Domestic Commerce and persuaded Congress to pass a bill in 1914 creating a system of commercial attachés, agents, and trade commissioners. Wilson encouraged foreign trade associations, telling the National Foreign Trade Convention in 1914 that "there is nothing in which I am more interested than the fullest development of the trade of this country and its righteous conquest of foreign markets." Bryan told businessmen that "my Department is your department." Wilson favored low tariffs mainly because without them other trading nations would raise tariffs against American goods. As Bryan said, "if we are to sell abroad, we must buy from people beyond our borders."

Outside Latin America, United States trade policies, though expansive, were not unfair. Wilson favored the "open door" and asked for no more than equal treatment. But south of the border it was quite otherwise. The United States had always claimed special rights there, and no one pressed them more insistently than Wilson. It must be said that he urged Congress to compensate Colombia for the loss of Panama. Yet Wilson also used force to establish brief American protectorates in Santo Domingo and Haiti, where much blood was shed. In 1916 Marines and gunboats, plus the threat of withholding loans, were used to elect a Nicaraguan president acceptable to American business. Wilson and Bryan had it both ways, as was the custom. They proclaimed the merits of Christian virtue, democracy, and exemplary American practices, at the same time using force to benefit American business interests.

To most Americans these were minor incidents. It was Mexico that tested Wilson's Latin-American policy most severely. The trouble began in 1911 when Mexican rebels overthrew their aged dictator Porfirio Diaz. Few outside Mexico minded this since it was thought to be just another coup. But the Mexican uprising was a real revolution, not just the replacement of one clique by another. The revolutionaries meant to free Mexico from domination by outside commercial interests while destroying such institutions as the landlords and the church, which they claimed kept 90 percent of the population in ignorance and poverty. This was bad news for capital because earlier, no matter who had been in office, money was always in power. Americans had a billion dollars invested in Mexico, more than in all the rest of the world. British investment was not so heavy, but was important all the same—especially to the Royal Navy, which got its oil from Mexico. When Wilson took office he assured a British envoy that he would straighten everything out. Specifically, he would "teach the South American republics to elect good men," establish a Mexican government "under which all contracts and business and concessions will be safer than they have been," and try to protect foreign property in Mexico during the revolution.

Wilson was in difficulty from the start because the reforming president of Mexico, Francisco Madero (1911–13), had just been murdered by General Victoriano Huerta, who now controlled the government. American investors in Mexico urged Wilson to recognize the new government immediately, something Taft had put off in the case of Madero, but Wilson refused. Wilson hoped that Huerta would be overthrown by Venustiano Carranza, a Maderista. To speed that happy day Wilson offered to mediate between Huerta and Carranza, both of whom astonished him by telling Wilson to mind his own business. Though wounded by this display of ingratitude, Wilson isolated the Huerta government diplomatically and induced Britain to stop selling arms to Huerta. And he allowed Carranza to buy arms in the United States, which Taft had forbidden. Huerta still obstinately refused to give up, forcing Wilson to search for a way of intervening directly. On April 10, 1914, he found his excuse. A party of American sailors loading supplies in Tampico were mistakenly arrested by Huertista authorities. They were soon released and apologies made to the American squadron commander, who declined to accept unless also given a twenty-one gun salute for Old Glory. Wilson backed him up on this. Mexico replied that it would comply if the salute was returned. Wilson refused, saying that to do so would be tantamount to recognizing the Huerta regime. For ten days nothing more happened; then Wilson got permission from Congress to use force in Mexico—the present custom of shooting first and seeking congressional approval afterward having not yet been adopted.

Wilson immediately ordered the squadron to take Veracruz, because a cargo of arms for Huerta was about to be landed there. On April 22 the city fell. The casualties were 126 Mexicans killed and 195 wounded, 19 Americans dead and 71 wounded. It was an easy victory that did Wilson no good, for Carranza was hardly less outraged than Huerta. Wilson wriggled on the hook awhile, then got off it when Argentina, Brazil, and Chile offered to mediate. That summer Huerta abdicated and Carranza took power. Things ought to have improved at this point but did not, for General Pancho Villa now turned against Carranza and the fighting resumed. Wilson proceeded to compound his earlier mistakes by almost supporting Villa, who was little more than a bandit.

The only explanation for this mistake, which Wilson barely avoided making in 1914, is that Villa was pro-American, the only Mexican leader on either side to applaud the storming of Veracruz. Vanity and pique thus led Wilson to flirt with a sure loser. In 1915, however, Wilson finally recognized the Carranza government, which was closing in on Villa. The next year, in a desperate effort to force American intervention, Villa started killing United States citizens and raiding American towns. The United States had just reached a hot-pursuit agreement with Mexico, giving either country the right to chase bandits across the border, so on March 15 a punitive exedition under General John J. Pershing went after Villa. Unfortunately, Carranza had not yet given his permission for the expedition to cross the border. Mexico had supposed the agreement meant only that small numbers of troops would cross over for limited periods of time. "Black Jack" Pershing had 5,000 men to start with and was soon 300 miles into Mexico, where the wily Villa hoped to lead him into a conflict with the Mexican army.

On June 18, 1916, Wilson mobilized some 100,000 National Guardsmen. On the 21st Mexican and American forces clashed, and Wilson seemed to be on the brink of war with Mexico despite himself. Although Wilson had meddled continuously in Mexican affairs from the beginning of his presidency, he had never wanted war. On the other hand, he clung to policies which made that prospect extremely likely. While assuring Carranza that the punitive expedition was meant only to destroy Villa, he refused to withdraw it when Carranza made repeated requests to that effect. Even after Mexican national forces began to concentrate in a way suggesting that Mexico expected war, Wilson stubbornly insisted on America's right to maintain a substantial force on Mexican soil indefinitely, though as some Americans pointed out had conditions been reversed the United States would never for a moment have tolerated lengthy stays on U.S. soil by foreign troops. Fortunately for Wilson, it soon became public knowledge that the incident of the 21st had been provoked by American troops. A flood of telegrams and letters, many organized by the pacifist American Union Against Militarism, together with numerous editorials, convinced him that few Americans wanted a war with Mexico.

Wilson did not then withdraw Pershing's forces, as might have been expected. But negotiations with the Carranza government were resumed. After Mexican national forces defeated Villa these bore fruit and in February, 1917, the punitive expedition was withdrawn. Wilson's Mexican adventures shed considerable light on his diplomacy. There is no question but that Wilson's intentions toward the Mexican people were honorable. He did not march into Mexico on the command of gold. He genuinely wanted to help Mexico obtain a legitimate constitutional government. Moreover, by effectively isolating the Huerta regime diplomatically, he assisted in its downfall. On the other hand, he committed serious errors, as in assaulting Veracruz and again in allowing the punitive expedition to go so deep into Mexico and remain so long. The parallel between his dealings with Mexico and Germany is far from exact, but in both cases without wanting war Wilson pursued high-minded policies so clumsily that they led to war, in the case of Germany, and to the brink of it with Mexico. Despite his good intentions Wilson had severe blind spots as a diplomatist, as his conduct of relations with Europe during World War I showed. For the most part, however, most Americans seemed to approve of his foreign policies until 1918 or 1919, and at home he moved from triumph to triumph.

THE NEW FREEDOM

Wilson's achievements at home resulted partly from the advantages he enjoyed on taking office in 1913. By then the public, having been prepared by years of political activity, was ready for certain kinds of changes. Congressional insurgents had reduced the Speaker of the House's power, weakening the old leadership and making things easier for a strong president. The opposition was divided between regulars and progressives. Democrats controlled both House and Senate. In 1913 Wilson's hand was all the stronger because 114 of the 290 Democrats in the House were first-termers who looked to him for guidance. The dominant figures in both parties were mostly progressive. And even conservative southern leaders felt that to stay in power the party had to attract dissident Republicans by enacting progressive measures.

Wilson played his hand skillfully. He dominated congressional Democrats from the start; paid close attention to the details of congressional business; conferred frequently with the leadership; and mediated intraparty disputes, using patronage when necessary to settle them. And if all else failed he could always appeal directly to a public opinion eager for reforms and susceptible to his oratory. In his inaugural address Wilson said: "This is not a day of triumph. It is a day of dedication. Here muster, not the forces of party, but the forces of humanity." Having declared himself to be above party, Wilson immediately showed himself to be a typical party leader, though shrewder than many. Wilson had not, it soon became clear, remained shackled to the naive and obsolete view of politics he had held as a professor. He worked with regular Democrats through men like Postmaster General Albert S. Burleson, who was especially close to southern leaders, and Bryan, who took care of the Midwest. Wilson's secretary of the treasury and future son-in-law, William G. McAdoo, was admired by younger liberals. Secretary of Labor William B. Wilson was a former trade unionist. The president's aide, Joseph Tumulty, was an Irish Catholic from Jersey City who talked the language of northern machine politicians. Colonel Edward M. House, who never held an office but was so influential that the president called him "my second personality," kept Wilson in touch with the rich and powerful, and with significant intellectuals. To strengthen what was still, despite the election of 1912, the minority party, Wilson compromised the civil service by giving Democratic regulars freedom to appoint their own men. Herbert Croly said he was the first president to lower the standards of federal employment since the civil service began. He also permitted federal employees in Washington to be racially segregated.

It did not take Wilson long to get action on reform measures. After taking office he called a special session of Congress to reform the tariff, an issue on which he had campaigned hard. Tariff reform was desired by farmers, who had to sell in a free market and buy in a protected one; by consumers, who disliked the high prices of protected goods; and even by many businessmen, who wanted to trade abroad and were handicapped by foreign tariffs that went up in response to American rate increases. In March, 1913, Democratic leaders brought forth the Underwood Tariff, which lowered duties on some manufactured goods but imposed duties on all farm products. Wilson told sponsoring Congressman Oscar W. Underwood to rewrite the bill and make food, sugar, leather, and wool free. Now the best tariff bill since the Civil War, it also provided for an income tax to make up what were expected to be revenue losses. Wilson and Bryan then jammed it through the House and fought a terrific battle in the Senate, where Republicans blocked it for months—some because the tariff rates were too low, others because the income tax was. In the end Wilson prevailed, accepting the higher income tax imposed by GOP insurgents and even lower duties than the House had voted. In its final version the Underwood Tariff reduced duties on the average from between 37 and 40 percent of value to about 26. The new tariff never had a chance to prove itself because the war interrupted normal trade and afterward the GOP pushed rates up again. All the same, it was a big victory for Wilson, showing that he had the power, knew how to use it, and meant to redeem his campaign promises. What followed was an array of new bills the like of which had not been seen in fifty years.

Some historians argue that Wilson had a well-developed ideology, shared with business leaders, that enabled him to make what has been called "corporate liberalism," or regulation for the sake of business, the dominant school of public thought in America. There is some truth to this so long as the term "ideology" is not taken too seriously. Wilson was anything but a disciplined or systematic thinker. He changed his mind too often on fundamentals to be a consistent ideologist. But he did have faith in the rightness of successful institutions, their viability being evidence that they conformed to natural laws. So while he believed in competition, he also came rather easily to believe in great corporations. Of them he said, "no man indicts natural history. No man undertakes to say that the things that have happened by operation of irresistible forces are immoral things. . . . " By 1912 he was convinced that the trusts were here to stay, that what they needed was not to be broken up but to be regulated so as to prevent their misuse by unscrupulous individuals. When it was pointed out to him that his views had come to resemble Roosevelt's, he remarked that he saw no difference between himself and a progressive Republican except that "he has a sort of pious feeling about the doctrine of protection, which I have never felt." Perhaps the chief difference was that Roosevelt seemed to think that entrepreneurs should throw in with the trusts, whereas Wilson thought there was room in the system for both. This explains Wilson's frequently quoted remark that he spoke for the "man on the make," rather than for the man who had it made. Wilson's principal bills, the Federal Reserve Act and the Federal Trade Commission Act, were meant to rationalize the outdated and inefficient structure within which business was done, while keeping big business honest and access to opportunity relatively open.

THE FEDERAL RESERVE ACT

Nothing better demonstrated the harmony of interest between Wilson and big business than the Federal Reserve Act of 1913. The

panic of 1907 had convinced nearly everyone of the need for banking reform. Many felt that the 7,000 banks in the country, some
chartered by Washington and others by the states, needed to be
standardized. All agreed there was not enough currency in circulation, especially to meet the seasonal needs of business and agriculture, and to avert panics by providing extra funds to banks in
emergencies. But ever since 1907 attempts to draw up a bill that
would please all the interested parties had failed. The so-called
Aldrich plan was favored by big banks because it featured a central
bank with fifteen branches that would determine discount rates,
issue currency, and perform other services under the direction of
bankers and businessmen. While the plan was intended to rationalize the banking situation, it was also aimed at helping large national
banks in New York fight off the competition.

For a time after the Civil War the national banks, which conformed to standards set by Washington, were unrivaled. Then state
banks, savings banks, and private banks began to increase. At the
same time New York's importance as a financial center declined. Its
share of the nation's total banking resources fell from 23 percent in
1902 to 18 percent in 1912. New York national bankers blamed their
relative decline on high standards. National banks had to maintain
larger reserves and take more precautions than other banks. They
naturally wanted to see everyone made to play by the same rules.
Banking reform to them meant improving their competitive position.

Nonnational banks were eager to retain their advantages. But
they had been shaken by the panic of 1907 too and wanted the
banking system strengthened. They also wanted a larger, more
flexible supply of currency. Despite the general sentiment for banking reform, it was hard to write a bill that did not offend some
important interest group. The Aldrich plan was blocked in Congress
because it called for a great central bank that Bryan Democrats were
sure would be putty in the hands of Wall Street. They wanted a
decentralized system, along with complete government control of
the currency, which most bankers were against. As large, small,
national, state, and private bankers all had different axes to grind it
was hard to get agreement among them, still less between them and
the Bryan Democrats in Congress. Wilson and Carter Glass, chairman of the House Banking Committee, finally decided to force the

issue. They wrote a bill that satisfied the need for more reserves, and the desire of small banks and agrarian Democrats for a decentralized system. It allowed the national banks to have foreign branches, something that would, Bryan said, "do more to promote trade in foreign lands than any other one thing that has been done in our history."

Progressives believed that in passing the Federal Reserve Act they were striking a blow against Wall Street. In fact, the big New York bankers got much of what they wanted in the end for two important reasons. First, Wilson gave big bankers three of the five seats on the first Federal Reserve Board, one of which went to Paul Warburg, who had written the Aldrich plan. Second, the New York Federal Bank gradually became the most important of the regional reserve banks, thus satisfying not only big New York bankers, but those who had wanted a single national bank rather than a decentralized system. In 1916 the New York District began acting for the entire system on foreign operations. It became the government's banker for all foreign transactions. From 1915 on New York bought securities for the entire system and handled all acceptances. Because the New York District was strongly led and the Federal Reserve Act loosely drawn, New York stabilized its position as a financial capital. And because becoming a national bank was now so much more attractive, state banks applied for national charters at a great rate. What the national banks had lost through business competition they regained through politics. No doubt given the conflicts of interest the only way to get the bank bill was to misrepresent it as Wilson did, to some extent. In any case the bill had real merits. It provided for a workable reserve system and an elastic currency. Eventually it functioned as a central bank, an institution sorely needed but lacking since the demise of Nicholas Biddle's Bank of the United States in 1836.

THE FEDERAL TRADE COMMISSION ACT

The Federal Trade Commission Act of 1914 was less a demonstration of presidential will than of presidential flexibility. Wilson wanted to satisfy the clamor against trusts in such a way as to help business. "I am for big business, and I am against the trusts," he had said. Once the tariff and banking problems were disposed of Wilson offered the Congress two measures. The Clayton bill would have prohibited various practices said to be unfair, and given labor some rights. The Covington bill would have established an interstate trade commission to investigate but not to regulate commerce. These bills satisfied no one. Big business did not want a bill outlawing practices that did not also establish a regulatory commission. Some tycoons were eager to have competition restricted. Labor wanted to be exempted from the Sherman Act. Agrarian progressives wanted concentrations of economic power broken up. Some progressives desired a bill that would rationalize the economy along New Nationalist lines.

Here again Wilson could not satisfy everyone. What he needed was a bill that would meet the desire of big business for regulated competition and the demand of antimonopoly forces for a blow against trusts. This could only be done through continuous regulation, which Wilson in his Jeffersonian period had opposed. Regulation had the great virtue of seeming to limit trusts while actually supporting them. However sternly its authors might insist that an FTC would police trusts, what mattered was how it was administered and by whom. Once Wilson decided on benevolent regulation he lost interest in the Clayton bill, which though finally enacted had little effect despite Samuel Gompers's claim that it was "labor's Magna Carta." Instead Wilson pushed a revised Federal Trade Commission bill through Congress that gave the FTC authority to define and enforce fair trade practices. Conservatives called it "socialistic," which it was not; radicals called it a "tool of big business," which it became. Like other regulatory agencies it was soon in bed with the very interests it was supposed to restrain. As always, one cannot be sure what Wilson wanted from the FTC. Perhaps he expected it to be independent, despite the proven tendency of government agencies to align themselves with the industries they were supposed to police. Some critics think the outcome of an action proves intent. Thus, when the FTC failed to enforce high standards they assumed it was meant to fail. But it is just as likely that Wilson was guilty of wishful thinking rather than calculation. Having passed his major bills Wilson then announced that the Republican system of special privilege had been ended and with it all animosity between business and the public. The age of reform was over. But Herbert Croly saw the FTC as more of a beginning than an end: "In this Trade Commission act is contained the possibility of a radical reversal of many American notions about trusts, legislative power, and legal procedure. It may amount to historic political and constitutional reform. It seems to contradict every principle of the party which enacted it."

Croly was nearer the mark than Wilson. Even though Wilson had been close to Roosevelt's program in 1912 there had been differences. Wilson retained a lingering affection for states' rights and Victorian business clichés. He was less committed to social justice. Wilson worried more about the constitutionality of humanitarian measures than about the problems they were meant to correct. He refused to support woman suffrage and child labor reform because he thought they violated states' rights. He openly favored racial segregation. In 1914 he vetoed a bill providing for long-term rural credits and almost vetoed the La Follette Seamen's Act of 1915. Thus, despite his skill as a parliamentary leader Wilson did not impress people as being either sophisticated or charitable. Actually, as both the banking and trade bills showed, Wilson had found a line which would meet business needs without seeming to do too much violence to his old principles, and which could be sold in Populist terms—even though agrarian progressives did not always buy it.

In practice the FTC, though sometimes a check on them, worked hand in glove with many business leaders. Edward N. Hurley, its strongest member, told the Association of National Advertisers in 1915 that the FTC was created to do for business in general what the ICC did for railroads and shippers, the Federal Reserve Board for bankers, and the Agriculture Department for farmers. Later he said that he was on the commission as a businessman who tried "to work wholly in the interest of business." Small business appreciated the information and other services rendered it by the FTC. More important, the FTC encouraged trade associations which tried to set prices and diminish competition. Big business profited too. In its first year the FTC launched ten helpful investigations. Hurley said of one that it was begun "with the hope that we can recommend to Congress some legislation that will allow them [coal companies] to combine and fix prices." Big business never did get a bill that would exempt companies from antitrust action once their mergers had been sanctioned by the FTC. But it did get the close and rewarding association with government it thought essential. There would still be antitrust actions, but not often and then usually in response to gross violations or public alarm. Wilson initiated fewer antitrust actions than Harding and Coolidge, though supposedly he was more hostile to business than they. The Federal Trade Commission Act demonstrated that the New Freedom was, to some extent, the New Nationalism, plus laissez-faire slogans.

SOCIAL LIBERALISM

Wilson finished his conversion two years later. In 1914 Democrats fared badly. The Progressive party collapsed and regular Republicans regained control of key states. The Democratic majority in the House fell from 75 to 25. Wilson had seemed to think that by meeting the business community's urgent need for banking and tariff reform, and for benevolent regulation, he would do himself much good. But while the president was esteemed by businessmen he won few of their votes. This meant that Wilson had to appeal to humanitarian progressives, who were the only large body of uncommitted voters. Once convinced of this Wilson moved with his usual energy. Of necessity he was now as certain that social justice was constitutional as he had been doubtful before. In January, 1916, Wilson appointed Louis Brandeis to the Supreme Court because of his identification with labor and social welfare. In May Wilson threw his support behind rural credits, speeding passage of the Federal Farm Loan Act. In August he endorsed child labor and federal workmen's compensation bills for the first time. He announced himself in favor of "rational protection," thus repudiating his old attachment to free trade. He pushed through the Adamson Act, giving railroad workers the eight-hour day, and said all workers should have it.

Wilson's strategy paid off. Many Progressives had been deeply hurt by the party's collapse and by Roosevelt's indifference to it after 1912. Once the war in Europe began Roosevelt lost interest in everything else and when Wilson refused to fight began sounding more and more demented. TR angled for the Republican nomination in 1916. When denied it he turned down the Progressive party nomination, telling the convention to name instead Senator Henry Cabot Lodge, who stood for everything Progressives were against. The Republican candidate, Charles Evans Hughes, campaigned against the Democrat's alleged inefficiency and Wilson's Mexican policy. To Hughes's barely concealed dismay TR helped out by stumping the country on behalf of militarism.

This did not leave Progressives with much choice. They had to prefer Wilson to Hughes. In consequence the *New Republic*, which Croly, Weyl, and Lippmann had established to promote the New Nationalism, went over to Wilson. So did such Progressive scholars as Charles Beard and John Dewey, and writers like Robert Herrick and Theodore Dreiser. The *New Republic* began calling its readers "liberal" instead of "progressive." Soon the latter term, because of its close association with the Progressive party of 1912, fell into disuse. "Liberal" became the usual name by which people who favored government intervention and/or social welfare were known. This was to cause much confusion as the two policies did not necessarily go hand in hand. Many businessmen were interventionists who wanted government help for themselves, while denying that the merely unfortunate had any claim on the public purse. It was also common for people to support welfare measures while rejecting government assistance to business.

Wilson's domestic policies fell short of what New Nationalists and humanitarian progressives desired. The economy was not rationalized and politicized. Many important social justice measures were not enacted. The New Freedom was not the New Deal. All the same, Wilson had moved a long way beyond his original nineteenth-century convictions, and his two terms witnessed significant steps toward the new view of government and its relation to the major interest groups that Croly and Roosevelt had advocated. For all his campaign rhetoric about the man on the make, Wilson accepted the great corporation as the basic unit of commercial life. Antitrust laws remained on the books, and in later years would sometimes even be invoked. But Wilson's administration made clear what has been basic national policy most of the time since then. Regulation, not laissez-faire or trust busting, is the keystone of government's relation to business, and regulation in practice confers more benefits on business than on the general public.

Wilson also committed government to protecting, however gradually, the interests of less fortunate Americans. This too marked a break with his past. As with his approach to corporations, it was not done because Wilson personally had a new revelation, but on account of political realities. Embracing social justice measures was to some degree the price of his reelection in 1916. Corporate liberalism and social liberalism were two sides of the same coin. The lesson of progressivism was that if laissez-faire was to be abandoned in favor of government intervention in, and supervision of, the economy, then it also had to be abandoned to some degree where humanitarian issues were concerned. Wilson's administration did not go as far in either direction as later ones would. But the New Freedom in this sense was the father of the New Deal, which extended corporate liberalism and social liberalism alike far beyond what most progressives had envisioned in Wilson's time. The Progressive era ended with many practices that we now take for granted still undeveloped. All the same, it drew in outline the basic relations between business, government, and the general public that exist today.

BIBLIOGRAPHICAL NOTES

By far the best work on Wilson is Arthur S. Link, *Wilson* (1947–   ), of which five volumes carrying the story up to 1917 have appeared. Link is extremely sympathetic to his subject and makes much of Wilson's alleged "idealism." All the same, Link's work is so rich and comprehensive that readers of any political persuasion should find it rewarding. A useful abbreviated work is Link's *Woodrow Wilson and the Progressive Era, 1910–1917* (1954). Link is also the editor of the *Papers of Woodrow Wilson*, a work which is expected to run to forty volumes. Two valuable books on relations with Mexico by Robert E. Quirk are *An Affair of Honor: Woodrow Wilson and the Occupation of Veracruz* (1962) and *The Mexican Revolution, 1914–1915* (1961). Link is especially good on the maneuvers leading up to the Federal Reserve Act and the Federal Trade Commission Act. For the opposite point of view see again Gabriel Kolko, *The Triumph of Conservatism* (1963). Wilson's appointment of Brandeis to the Supreme Court was highly controversial, both because Brandeis was disliked by big business and because he was the first Jew named to the high court. This incident is discussed in Alden L. Todd, *Justice on Trial* (1964). Labor's experiences are dealt with in Philip Taft, *The A.F.L. in the Time of Gompers* (1957).

7

AND THE WAR CAME

For all its faults, the Progressive era was as exciting and creative as any in American history. In poetry, fiction, architecture, the dance, and other arts foundations were laid for structures that would make America a cultural great power. Politicians displayed more originality and responsiveness than before. The new, even the radical, got a fairer hearing than Victorians would have allowed. Probably more bills relating to social welfare were passed, especially on the state and local level, than in the whole of American history before 1900. Then Wilson, who had hoped his administration would culminate the age of reform, instead destroyed it by going to war.

This was inadvertent on Wilson's part. Unlike Roosevelt he did not enjoy making foreign policy. And, unlike Roosevelt again, he deplored violence. Wilson never killed anyone. If he had he would not have boasted of it as Roosevelt did. When the Great War broke out it seemed unlikely at first that Wilson's principles would be severely tested. Though a majority of Americans probably supported the Allies, no one wanted to enter the holocaust except a handful of warmongers like TR. Because he admired the Kaiser and German efficiency it took Roosevelt a few weeks to decide which side he was on. Once pledged to the Allies, though, he worked for American intervention with a fervor bordering on lunacy. When Wilson obstinately refused to make war against Germany Roosevelt called him "exceedingly base" and said his soul was "rotten through and through." The public's enthusiasm in 1916 for the slogan "He kept us out of war" showed it to be "yellow." After American entry Roosevelt attacked socialism, pacifism, pornography, free love, and the German language. He supported nativism, superpatriotism, and, though he condemned mob violence, fed the lynching spirit by hysterically abusing dissenters.

But until 1917 Roosevelt was in the minority. Most Americans took it for granted that the war proved European civilization to be decadent, imperialistic, reactionary, and hardly worth saving. Despite a considerable sympathy for the Allies, there was no question of American entry until 1916 at the earliest. Even the great capitalists, later to be branded as "merchants of death," were far from agreed that an Amerian war effort would be good for business. They welcomed the Allied orders that poured in after 1914. But while happy to profit from the war few Americans wanted to share its dangers. Americans were exceedingly pacifistic in theory during the Progressive era. Numerous peace societies had been formed. Andrew Carnegie, who had always been a pacifist (even in business, though he sold armor plate to the navy, it was defective), created a great endowment for international peace. It was a truism among middle-class Americans that civilization, at least their own, had evolved beyond war. Another was that given modern weapons, warfare was so dangerous that no sane people would embark on it—for long anyway.

This meant that Wilson was under little pressure to intervene, or to react violently when America's rights as a neutral were violated by both sides—so long as America's foreign trade was not seriously impaired. Even after the *Lusitania* was sunk in 1915 he could still resist cries for action with the fatuous remark that "there is such a thing as a man being too proud to fight." Yet though Wilson had urged Americans to be entirely neutral when war broke out, he was pro-Ally at heart and made crucial decisions, usually without much thought, that led gradually to intervention. When Britain unilaterally declared that most exports to Germany were contraband the United States objected, but not so strenuously as to make any difference. Britain mined the North Sea, ignoring a feeble and belated American protest. When Britain began arming its merchantmen, Germany said this made them warships and hence barred from neutral ports according to international law. The United States decided instead that the merchantmen were arming themselves against piracy and so were eligible to use American ports. From Germany's point of view these decisions compromised American neutrality at the outset. Wilson seemed to think it was possible to cooperate with the Allies without being aligned with them. This distinction eluded the Germans, who never believed in American neutrality after the fall of 1915. And America was not strictly neutral, as Wilson's position on loans showed. When the war began Washington forbade private loans to belligerents. In October, 1914, Wilson let it be known that this ban did not extend to interbank credits. The distinction between loans and credits, so vital to the American definition of neutrality, also eluded Berlin.

AMERICA MOVES TOWARD INTERVENTION

A crucial turning point was reached early in 1915 when Germany began using submarines against merchant shipping. This was the fateful issue that finally led to American intervention. In those innocent days submarines, because they were as dangerous to civilians as to combatants, were thought the last word in barbarism. But as Britain still ruled the waves submarines were the only naval weapons Germany could use. Bryan realized this and got Wilson to suggest a deal. If Germany recalled its submarines Britain was to strike foodstuffs off the contraband list. Germany seemed agreeable if the British blockade was further limited to war materials only. In effect this would have ended the blockade, for Germany made its own munitions. What Germany needed were the raw materials denied it by British seapower. However, Britain saw no reason to lift the blockade merely because Germany was willing to recall twenty-eight submarines of, at the time, doubtful effectiveness and ignored the Wilson proposal. Wilson let this pass, and so lost the best chance to remain neutral. Had the exhange gone through in some form the main reason for America's ultimate intervention would have vanished.

In the war's first year several British ships went down with Americans on board. Then on May 7, 1915, the British liner *Lusitania* was torpedoed at a cost of 1,198 lives, 128 of them American. There was a great outcry at this, even though the *Lusitania* had been armed, carried munitions, had been known to fly the American flag, and therefore could not claim the protection of international law. Secretary of State Bryan wanted to avoid a showdown with Germany and to insist that both belligerents respect neutral rights, which to his mind did not include the right to travel on belligerent vessels without getting hurt. Wilson, under heavy pressure from jingoes, demanded that Germany call off its U-boats at once. Bryan then resigned, showing great courage as it ended his career in public life. Wilson and the Germans each backed down slightly thereafter. Wilson stopped asking for a complete end to submarine warfare. The Germans finally gave the "Arabic Pledge," saying they would no longer attack liners of any nation without warning. This solved the crisis but settled nothing. The status of merchantmen remained unclear. By sticking his head out Wilson invited the Germans to cut it off. If they unleashed their U-boats again Wilson would have to declare war or lose a politically unacceptable amount of face.

Another fateful, though little noticed, step toward war came in the fall of 1915. Because the Allies were running out of cash private American bankers asked that the ban on direct loans to belligerents be ended. Without private loans, it was argued, Allied spending in the United States would fall, causing unemployment, unrest, and a Democratic defeat at the next election. This was probably true, so in October, 1915, Wilson told Wall Street to go ahead. By the time America intervened private bankers had loaned the Allies nearly $4 billion.

Wilson toyed with the idea of mediation, but did little to prepare himself for it. When more Americans suffered from U-boat attacks, Wilson forced the German government to give, on May 4, 1916, the "Sussex Pledge." This was a promise to visit and search all vessels

before sinking them. The pledge drastically reduced U-boat operations, but was conditional on America's insistence that Britain observe the rules of war, that is, confine her blockade to genuine
contraband. Since Britain was unlikely to comply, the effectiveness
of the Sussex Pledge could not last long.

The pledge bought time, which Wilson tried to employ usefully.
In December, 1916, he asked both sides to state their war aims,
hoping they would not be so far apart as to preclude negotiations.
Germany no longer trusted Wilson, though at this point he seems to
have been sincere, and delayed its answer. The Allied reply listed
terms even Wilson thought unreasonable. He knew that Europe
needed peace more than the powers needed victory. Later the great
diplomat and diplomatic historian George Kennan would say that
any of the belligerents would have been better off to surrender in
1916, than to win in 1918. The war's cost was becoming so great that
no triumph could possibly make up for what both sides were losing.
Wilson suggested as much in his justly famous peace-without-
victory speech to the Senate on January 22, 1917. But none of the
powers dared to make peace so long as there remained a chance,
however slight, of prevailing. This was not chiefly a matter of greed,
though each side meant to force the other to pay all the war's costs.
Politicians rejected a negotiated peace because they felt the people
would not stand for it. Europeans were thought to be mad for
revenge, ready to turn out any government that did not redeem
their suffering with victory. And the rich of all countries at the very
least wanted reparations from their enemies to pay off their own war
loans, believing the alternative would be enormous postwar taxes.

Wilson could not become a mediator unless he used force or the
threat of it. Since the Allies needed American goods and loans, the
fear of losing them might have brought England and France to the
conference table. Germany might have negotiated in 1916 if the
alternative had been American intervention on the Allied side. But
these possibilities were never considered. Too many prominent
Americans, including all of Wilson's key advisers, were pro-Allied.
They would never allow an interruption in Anglo-American trade.
Though Wilson was willing to threaten Germany with war over
neutral rights, he could not do so merely for the sake of peace, as any
such threat would have to include England as well.

DECLARATION OF WAR

Wilson's overtures came too late in any event. Germany had already decided to renew the U-boat campaign when he gave his peace-without-victory speech. On January 31, 1917, Wilson was notified that undersea operations would resume the following day. Wilson then spent the next two months fidgeting and praying for guidance. Perhaps he hoped public opinion, which was sharply divided, would coalesce. It did not, though elite businessmen, intellectuals, and publishers seem to have largely agreed that war was necessary, if only to end the suspense. Wilson's cabinet thought so too. Wilson called Congress into session and on April 2 asked it to declare war. Though a handful, led by Senator La Follette in his finest hour, refused, most congressmen clapped and cheered. Afterward Wilson told his secretary: "My message today was a message of death for our young men. How strange it seemed to applaud that." Wilson was properly stricken at what he had done. The president never wanted war. He asked for it because a long string of missed opportunities, acts prejudicial to Germany, and his conviction that Americans had a right to sail safely on British ships in wartime and businessmen to ship through combat zones left him with no alternative. To some degree Wilson knew he was responsible for the men who would die. Yet this did not have a mellowing effect on his character. To the contrary, Wilson was determined that the lives lost would not be wasted. To prevent that he would suffer no critics, tolerate no resistance, and accept no blame for whatever went wrong. Anything else would have risked having the dead on his conscience, an intolerable prospect for such a man as Wilson.

America made war chiefly to protect its maritime rights. As this was not a very impressive reason grander ones had to be found. National honor was an obvious choice. But even honor was too small a reason for the president, though he had to be conscious of it. In his war message Wilson seized the highest possible ground, arguing that German violations of neutral rights was a challenge to all mankind. The United States would go to war to "vindicate the principles of peace and justice in the life of the world as against selfish and autocratic power and to set up amongst the really free and self-governing people of the world such a concert of purpose and of

action as will henceforth ensure the observance of those principles."
Wilson insisted that the German government had a monopoly on
wickedness, calling it "this natural foe to liberty" (no mention here
that England was at the very moment denying liberty to Ireland and
India). Another theme was that the world "must be made safe for
democracy." War was terrible, he went on, "but the right is more
precious than peace, and we shall fight for the things which we have
always carried nearest our hearts"—democracy, self-determination,
"a universal dominion of right by such a concert of free peoples as
shall bring peace and safety to all nations and make the world itself at
last free."

As the Allies had no intention of freeing the hundreds of millions
of people in their colonial empires this was nonsense, but such bold
nonsense that Wilson got away with it. Perhaps nothing less would
have inspired the nation to discard its prejudice against foreign
military alliances. American diplomacy, moments of hysteria notwithstanding, was practical, low-key, and interest-oriented. Americans believed in going it alone. Now Wilson summoned them to
make war with other powers for objects so elevated and fanciful that
no sensible person ought to have taken them seriously. But conditions were such that millions did, including Wilson's enemies like
Senator Henry Cabot Lodge, who thanked the president after his
war message for having expressed the loftiest sentiments of the
American people. Intervention had an astonishing effect on many
intellectuals, academicians, and social workers. After having talked
against intervention, sometimes for years, masses of them suddenly
discovered that the war was not a stupid bloodbath after all, but a
crusade to remake the world along progressive lines.

There was little criticism of Wilson's vague pronouncements from
quarters where it might have been expected. The *New Republic*,
which may have coined the phrase "peace without victory," was so
excited when Wilson used it that the magazine claimed that liberal
intellectuals were responsible for intervention—a conceit Wilson
nourished at small cost to himself by having Colonel House meet
with Croly and Lippmann. Contrary to liberal myths, once war was
declared all power devolved on the military and the executive, both
much more influenced by businessmen than by intellectuals. Randolph Bourne mocked intellectuals for thinking they were "gently
guiding a nation through sheer force of ideas into what the other

nations entered only through predatory craft or popular hysteria or militarist madness! A war free from any taint of self-seeking, a war that will secure the triumph of democracy and internationalize the world!"

Bourne and other pacifists knew that Wilson's claims for American intervention were absurd for two reasons. The first was that America went to war not out of high-mindedness, but to protect her maritime rights, perhaps also the huge American investment in an Allied victory. If the Allies lost they might not repay what they owed Americans. The success of German U-boats, and the decline of Russia, suggested that Germany might prevail. Preventing this was the fundamental American war aim. Second, even if Wilson really wanted universal peace and freedom, by going to war he made certain they would not be gained. As he had said, only a peace without victory, a peace between equals had a chance of lasting. This might have been accomplished by a limited naval war, which would have defended American rights without destroying Germany. To crush Germany was to risk another war when Germany regained its strength. As Wilson said, an imposed peace "would be accepted in humiliation, under duress, at an intolerable sacrifice, and would leave a sting, a resentment of bitter memory upon which terms of peace would rest, not permanently, but only as upon quicksand."

Wilson's manner of joining the war also meant the end of an independent American course of action. Wilson made no effort to commit the Allies to his grand scheme, though he knew that if the Allies won they would be greedy. He saved them without exacting any concessions beforehand. They desperately needed American supplies, and as it turned out, American troops. America gave generously of both with no thought of the morrow. When the war was over the United States had no pledges of good behavior from the Allies and no way of getting them. Bourne could see what was happening as early as August, 1917, when he published his brilliant essay "The Collapse of American Strategy." But all through the war Wilson and his friendly intellectuals operated as if Britain and France would do as they wanted afterward. They all shared the same delusions. They seemed to think that such splendid ends would somehow create their own means, which only shows how much self-deception bright men are capable of if they apply themselves.

CONVINCING THE PUBLIC

Because American opinion was so divided, despite Wilson's war message, an intensive propaganda campaign was thought necessary. But the need for a government agency to generate it was not overwhelmingly apparent even if one liked propaganda. On their own newspapers began a tremendous anti-German effort once war was declared, announcing the discovery of a "Teuton Plan to Torture Captured Sammies" and similar fantasies. A Committee on Public Information was quickly formed anyway, and a progressive journalist, George Creel, made its head. The CPI turned out an enormous volume of material; its scholarship division alone produced seventy-five million pieces of literature. On a higher level this consisted of essays by Carl Becker and other distinguished historians showing how German ideas were responsible for all the world's problems. Academicians also explained how the war was being fought on behalf of American workers, who ought, therefore, to give up strikes for the duration.

On a lower level the scholarship division of the CPI sponsored ads in college newspapers. One said: "In the vicious guttural language of Kultur [German culture], the degree A.B. means Bachelor of Atrocities. Are you going to let the Prussian Python strike at your Alma Mater as it struck at the University of Louvain? The Hohenzollern fang strikes at every element of decency and culture and taste that your college stands for." When not corrupting decency, culture, and taste on college campuses, the CPI helped promote films like *The Prussian Cur* and *The Kaiser, the Beast of Berlin*. The movie industry also produced uplifting pictures such as *Pershing's Crusaders*. *Our Colored Fighters* was aimed at black morale, a problem because black soldiers were confined mostly to segregated labor battalions.

The CPI turned out daily news bulletins, cartoons, syndicated features, and posters. Its corps of speakers, called Four-Minute Men, gave canned talks in theaters, churches, schools, and anywhere else crowds of two or more people could be assembled. Much of this propagandizing was innocuous, but some of it was not; for example, the ad urging citizens to "report the man who spreads pessimistic stories, divulges—or seeks—confidential military information, cries for peace, or belittles our efforts to win the war." Send names to the

Justice Department, it went on. "Show the Hun we can beat him at his own game. . . ." The ad promised to keep the identity of informers secret. This policy, though hardly in keeping with the spirit of Wilson's lofty war aims, worked very well. At one time the government was receiving 1,500 accusations a day, though the number of German spies and saboteurs in America was negligible.

While odious in its own right, the CPI was only part of the national effort to abolish discontent by force. Laws were passed, notably the Espionage Act of 1917 and the Espionage Act (often called the Sedition Act) of 1918, which provided penalties of up to twenty years in prison for obstructing the draft, making false reports in aid of the enemy, expressing unwanted opinions, and much else. Although little remained of the Bill of Rights once these laws had been passed, most prominent Americans defended them—excluding Theodore Roosevelt, who in self-defense had to oppose the Sedition Act because it made verbally abusing the president, something Roosevelt did every day, a crime. Roosevelt got away with such attacks but thousands did not. The great anarchists Emma Goldman and Alexander Berkman were early casualties of the witch-hunt. In Rockford, Ill., 150 Wobblies and Socialists were given sentences of up to twenty years after a four-hour trial. Kate Richards O'Hare, past national secretary of the Socialist party, got five years in prison for criticizing the war. Eugene Debs was sent to Atlanta Penitentiary for the same reason. An elderly South Dakota farmer was given five years for urging a local boy not to enlist. Wobbly and Socialist headquarters were raided frequently.

Academic freedom, a tenuous concept at best in those days, was suspended everywhere but at Harvard University. The American Association of University Professors issued a report saying it was the duty of universities to ensure the patriotism of their faculties. Though only fourteen professors are known to have been fired for disliking the war, there is no way to tell how many did not get their contracts renewed, or were not hired to begin with, for their views. Public school teachers lost their jobs too. In New York a teacher was fired for discussing anarchism in a neutral manner, rather than condemning it out of hand as patriotism required. A Maine school teacher was let go for taking driving lessons from a German immigrant. Preachers were equally vulnerable. A Methodist school superintendent was fired for refusing to give prowar addresses.

Some ministers, pacifists as a rule, went to prison. In Los Angeles three were beaten by a mob and then arrested for expressing "thoughts and theories . . . calculated to cause any American citizen then and there present to assault and batter" them. They were sentenced to six months in jail and fined $1,500. Wilson encouraged the punishment of malcontents. In 1918 he asked his attorney general to "bring to book" the editor of the *Kansas City Star* for publishing a letter from a prominent Socialist, Rose Pastor Stokes, that said "the government is for the capitalists." The attorney general did not think this actionable. But Mrs. Stokes went to prison for giving the speech her letter was meant to clarify.

While the government's campaign was bad enough, the popular response was even worse. Aliens were beaten on the streets, German immigrants compelled to buy war bonds and tormented in many ways. Radicals, being already under attack by the government, were fair game. Socialist rallies and marches were broken up. Members of the IWW, which, unlike the Socialist party, had not formally denounced the war, suffered still more as there was more to be gained from assaulting them. In Bisbee, Ariz. where the IWW was organizing metal workers, vigilantes kidnapped 1,200 strikers and dumped them in the New Mexico desert. Even the *New York Times,* then in a fiercely nationalistic phase, thought this was going too far. But no one was ever brought to book for depriving the Wobblies of their rights. Frank Little, a legendary Wobbly organizer, was tortured and hanged by vigilantes in Butte, Mont. After the Justice Department raided thirty-three IWW headquarters in September, 1917, mob attacks on Wobblies became common.

When blacks began moving North to work in defense industries they were attacked by racial bigots. The worst riot was in East St. Louis, where white mobs attacked black districts killing 40 blacks and destroying 300 homes. As in the South, torture and mutilation were freely employed. These and lesser outrages prompted black leaders to request a meeting with the president, which was denied. Later he issued a feeble statement to the effect that massacre was unsporting, perhaps even un-American. Drafting blacks into the army caused problems too. They were segregated and humiliated in the service as in civilian life. Citizens and policemen in the towns where black soldiers went for recreation harassed them. Black troops finally exploded in Houston and attacked a jail where some comrades were being held prisoner. Fifteen people died in the assault. Afterward the army held a drumhead court-martial. Forty-one black soldiers were sentenced to life imprisonment and thirteen were hanged in an arroyo outside the camp.

The draft law exempted men who were conscientious objectors on religious grounds. The problem was that COs were put in the army's charge, and the army believed they were all slackers—that is, cowards who were afraid to fight—and tried to make them accept military service. Of some 20,000 COs who reported to army camps with certificates of exemption, in the end 16,000 accepted some kind of military duty. This was accomplished often by beating, imprisoning, and otherwise maltreating the COs. Those who held out despite everything were usually members of traditional pacifist sects like the Mennonites and Dukhobors, whom the army despised. They were often forcibly shaven, though obliged by their religion to wear beards, and made to wear uniforms, which was also against their religion. Some died of abuse. The army went on thinking it was brave to sign up, even when doing so was against your principles, and cowardly to refuse, even at the risk of your life. Four hundred and fifty COs were court martialed on one pretext or another. Seventeen were sentenced to death, 142 to life imprisonment, and 345 to sentences averaging sixteen years in length. None of the death sentences appear to have been carried out, though an undetermined number of COs committed suicide.

The war meant a reign of terror at home, and the practice of all those evils that Allied propaganda held to be peculiarly German. No one except the victims seemed to notice this. Too many Americans were busy having a good time. There were some exceptions: 50,000 Americans were killed in action, and 75,000 more died of illness, most of them from an influenza epidemic that carried off ten million people around the world; 200,000 soldiers were wounded, but 85 percent of them were returned to duty thanks to new medical advances that enabled physicians for the first time to do their war-casualty patients more good than harm. The average soldier did not get hurt or see much combat. Large numbers of American troops were in the trenches only during the last eight months of war.

Women's clubs, and even some feminist organizations, threw themselves into war work, rolling bandages, driving official cars, saving food, and selling bonds, at which they proved so adept that official agencies competed for their services. Some women went to work for the first time to relieve manpower shortages; many more moved up to better paying jobs vacated by men. Men and women alike found excitement and satisfaction in the host of new agencies, public and private, that were developed or enlarged on account on the emergency. It was thrilling that everyone joined together to advance civilized values—or nearly everyone. There were disloyal and un-American elements—Socialists, pacifists, "hyphenated Americans" (meaning immigrants, especially from the Central Powers). And there were men too cowardly or subversive to accept the draft. Hundreds of thousands refused to register or be inducted. The army tried to catch them by cordoning off city blocks and demanding to see every man's draft card. The dragnet was so unpopular it had to be dropped, thus becoming the only war practice that public opinion was effectively mobilized against. Despite these numerous exceptions most people went on thinking the war had united them. This feeling of shared purposes, though false, would be missed afterward. Even when people turned against the war effort later, they would remember fondly their experiences during it.

MOBILIZATION ALONG PROGRESSIVE LINES

Suppressing dissent was a small part of the war effort. Contemporaries attached far less weight to it than historians have since. At the time the mobilization of national resources, human and material, seemed far more important. In this effort human needs received greater attention than social reformers had expected. Though many of the reformers had been pacifists most accepted the decision to intervene. Still, they feared that the health and welfare of the people would suffer, and consequently they geared up to protect such gains as had already been achieved. Their worries were unfounded. From the start Washington asked their advice and often took it. There were several reasons for this. England's experience had demonstrated that overworking employees in defense plants and neglecting safety standards hurt production. So Washington appointed Samuel Gompers to the Council of National Defense and pushed for the eight-hour day. In its own manufacturing arsenals the government maintained high labor standards. Elsewhere abuses took place. However, these were not worse than in peacetime, and frequently were less severe, as the government threatened to make war orders contingent on good labor practices and safety measures. Agencies like the War Labor Board and the War Labor Policies Board did a good deal to enhance labor's position and minimize the exploitation of working women and children. Critics said that Washington was buying off workers with modest concessions while ignoring fundamental inequities between capital and labor. This was true, yet while conditions fell short of what labor leaders would have liked, working people were still better off than otherwise. Not surprisingly, most union chiefs felt that half a loaf was better than none.

Other social problems were ameliorated too. The government built or controlled dozens of housing projects for war workers during the emergency according to standards set by Lawrence Veiller, dean of progressive housing reformers. Advocates of social insurance were heartened by passage of the Military and Naval Insurance Act of 1917, which was drawn up with the aid of such reformers as Lee Frankel and Julia Lathrop. Some authorities believed there was more improvement in public health during the first year of war than in the previous ten years. Community councils and war chests, which raised money for the emergency, led to federated fund drives that supported local service agencies afterward.

Nothing impressed social welfare people more during the war than the way military training camps were handled. Secretary of War Newton Baker and Raymond Fosdick, both veteran reformers, established a Commission on Training Camp Activities which applied the techniques of social work, recreational planning, and community organization to military posts. In effect, as Allen F. Davis says, they meant to surround each camp with a social settlement. To a remarkable degree this is what happened. American soldiers and sailors during World War I were lavishly provided with health, welfare, and recreational opportunities, especially by comparison with earlier conflicts. The handling of sex problems was exceptionally thorough. In earlier wars they had been largely ignored. This was not the progressive way. As antibiotics had not yet been invented, venereal disease was a threat to military efficiency. It was also the result of immoral conduct. Progressives were against it on both counts and tried hard to keep prostitutes away from the training camps. Brothels were closed and red-light districts abolished.

Horrifying movies on the effect of VD were shown to inspire fear among those with whom all else had failed. Innocent recreations vented feelings that might otherwise have found rowdier expression. The Military Draft Act prohibited the sale of liquor to men in uniform. Raymond Fosdick led efforts to abolish sin in the services with the motto "Fit to Fight."

All this produced what was called the "cleanest army since Cromwell's day," whether the men liked it or not. Even going abroad did not help lustful soldiers as much as they may have hoped. Overseas forces were forbidden to drink hard liquor or visit French brothels, which Clemenceau thoughtfully volunteered to make available for American use. When Fosdick revealed this offer to Baker the secretary replied, "for God's sake, Raymond, don't show this to the President or he'll stop the war." The military, if more virtuous than they cared to be, were also more battle-ready. In few other areas did the twin objects of progressive enthusiasm, virtue and efficiency, find better expression.

To New Nationalists these health and welfare measures, though welcome, were peripheral. What mattered was the accomplishing of industrial mobilization along lines they had suggested earlier. Just as the war suspended opposition to prohibition and other social reforms, so too did it reduce the prejudice against centralized economic controls. The European experience allowed people to take for granted what would have been unthinkable in peacetime. This was understood even before American entry, as shown by Wilson's creation of the Committee on Industrial Preparedness in 1916. Late in the year it was replaced by the Council of National Defense. Its Advisory Commission, which actually ran the CND, included Secretary of the Treasury McAdoo, a former railroad promoter; Walter S. Gifford, formerly chief statistician of AT&T; the president of the Baltimore and Ohio Railroad; Bernard Baruch, the renowned financier; and Julius Rosenwald, whc was president of Sears, Roebuck. The CND promoted closer relations between business and government, and set up committees of businessmen to regulate sales and prices. The main instrument of what Murray Rothbard has called "war collectivism" was the War Industries Board, which coordinated government purchases, allotted commodities, and fixed prices and priorities. In March, 1918, Baruch took over the WIB and became, as was said, the "autocrat" of the

American economy. The WIB was organized into "commodity sections" run by big businessmen who gave out contracts as they saw fit, with no competitive bidding. There was little concern with efficiency and costs, though in theory management by trained executives was supposed to increase the first and diminish the second.

Business enthusiasm for war collectivism resulted from the fact that prices were stabilized, market fluctuations ironed out, and prices set by mutual consent of government and industry. Some smaller firms resented the end of competition because they would have made even more money without controls. Even so, profits were large enough to content all but the greediest.

Unlike World War II most foodstuffs were not rationed, though some controls were imposed. Herbert Hoover's Food Administration licensed food producers and distributors, thus enforcing compliance. A voluntary network of citizens monitored the food industry to make sure directives were observed. Prices were set to ensure a "reasonable" profit. The Food Administration's Grain Corporation bought most of the wheat crop and sold it to millers, guaranteeing that each firm would be maintained in the same position relative to its competitors throughout the war. In effect, this cartelized the milling industry. The International Sugar Committee bought the entire Cuban sugar crop at reduced rates. When Cuba balked, America curtailed the export of bread, flour, and coal, and Cuba soon gave way. This tactic was self-defeating, however. Low prices encouraged people to eat more sugar, which then had to be rationed.

Railroads were nationalized, except for profits. The Railroad Administration managed the roads and promised their owners that the high profit levels of 1916–17 would be maintained. This was especially gratifying because the Interstate Commerce Commission was then in the hands of shipping interests, who, save for the RA, would have probably gotten reduced charges. The RA was dominated by railroad men, who in 1918 raised shipping rates by 25 percent while reducing services.

War collectivism was not universally popular. Shippers naturally resented the Railroad Administration. The best-managed companies disliked administered prices. All the same, those who favored a managed economy felt that aspects of collectivism should continue after the war. "Socialism for the rich" had proven to be good business. Baruch was an active champion of economic direction. Rail-roaders hoped that the RA would be maintained in some form. The WIB wanted to perpetuate itself. The National Chamber of Commerce called a Reconstruction Congress of American Industry after the war which declared that the Sherman Act ought to be amended to allow restrictive trade agreements. The National Association of Manufacturers, previously devoted to competition, agreed. Despite this show of strength corporate collectivists were disappointed at first. Wilson still believed in competition to a degree. The end of the emergency revived traditional prejudices against combination. War-time agencies were abolished. Railroads were put back in the hands of reluctant owners. Still, these experiences were remembered. When the Great Depression struck some liberals argued that it was an emergency like the war and required similar methods. Many New Dealers were admirers of the war system. The National Recovery Administration, President Roosevelt's first major attempt at recovery, was based on wartime precedents.

MAKING PEACE

Wilson's doomed effort to remake the world is too long and complex a story to tell here, though a brief mention must be made of it. During the war, as before, Wilson was borne along by events. He did receive assurances of good conduct after the war from the Allies and maintained the fiction that America was not tied to them by calling the United States an "Associated Power," rather than an ally. The Fourteen Points which induced Germany to sign an armistice were unilaterally proclaimed by Wilson. They bound no one, not even the United States. The armistice terms (German withdrawal beyond the Rhine, the surrender of its arms) were such that Germany could not resume fighting even had it wished to. This removed the last check on Allied rapacity.

Arthur Link has said that Wilson was the only realist at Versailles because he alone knew that fair terms were essential to a lasting peace. But Wilson was in a poor position to enforce his point. Having failed to exact agreements from the Allies when they needed him, why should he have expected compliance when they did not? Another sense in which Wilson might be called realistic had to do with the way he defined a just peace. As outlined in the Fourteen

Points it meant that the seas were to be free in peace and war, armaments were to be reduced, free trade assured, national rights guaranteed, and a world assembly established that would be dominated by what Wilson called the "great white nations." These principles were to the advantage of most countries, especially America. The League of Nations excepted, they were traditional American goals. America was the only great capitalist power without a great colonial empire, or the large permanent military establishment needed to protect one. Accordingly, it was in its interest to promote disarmament, free trade, and open seas. They cost America nothing while creating an international climate in which she might do business on the best possible terms. These conditions, if established, would have benefited smaller nations too, enabling Americans to say that in promoting them the United States was acting selflessly. This irritated the Allies without changing their minds.

Though the peace treaty fell far short of what Americans expected, the war left America in a good position anyway. Its main economic competitors were exhausted and in debt. This would have been the case in any event, so little credit for its postwar prosperity can be attached to America's intervention. The American position after the war was much the same as if the country had not fought at all. When Wilson went to Versailles he bargained away many points that victory was supposed to secure on the theory that a League of Nations would redeem all failures. This was a thin hope, even before the Senate dashed it by refusing to confirm the peace treaty. The Senate rejected the treaty for partisan reasons, and out of pique at not being consulted. Some senators felt it was a counterrevolutionary document unsuited to an age of revolutions. Wilson refused to compromise and destroyed himself politically and physically by trying to reverse this judgment.

Wilson's tragedy was a personal one and made little difference to the country. Continuing to pursue national interests abroad, though less theatrically, America prospered at Europe's expense. Wilson's partisans bemoaned the brave new world that never would be, thanks to European perfidy and Republican shortsightedness. The war having failed to produce what no sane person ought to have expected of it was disowned, and the blame for it assigned to merchants of death and other scapegoats. Americans resolved not to intervene in Europe again, which made for problems when the next war came along, as people often failed to see the difference between it and World War I. Many bitter novels were written to the effect that war was hell. This was what the country had to show for the $33.5 billion and 50,000 lives it invested in victory.

BIBLIOGRAPHICAL NOTES

Besides Link, see Ernest R. May, *The World War and American Isolation* (1959), for a good if conventional treatment of the struggle over intervention. There is valuable material in Robert E. Osgood, *Ideals and Self-Interest in America's Foreign Relations* (1953), and in George F. Kennan, *American Diplomacy, 1900–1950* (1951). The most lively revisionist account taking issue with the original justifications for American entry is Walter Millis, *Road to War: America, 1914–1917* (1935). Bourne's great antiwar essays are available in Randolph S. Bourne, *War and the Intellectuals* (1964), Carl Resek, ed. The standard work is H. C. Peterson and G. C. Fite, *Opponents of War, 1917–1918* (1957). A full description of wartime progressivism is Chapter 11, "World War I and After," in Allen F. Davis, *Spearheads of Reform* (1967). A contemporary revisionist study is N. Gordon Levin, Jr., *Woodrow Wilson and World Politics* (1968), which sees Wilson as systematically trying to create a "stable world order of liberal-capitalist internationalism." Though overdrawn, this is an intelligently argued radical critique of Wilsonianism. A brilliant if not always convincing essay from the same viewpoint is Martin J. Sklar, "Woodrow Wilson and the Political Economy of Modern United States Liberalism," in Ronald Radosh and Murray Rothbard, eds., *A New History of Leviathan* (1972). Another suggestive leftist analysis is James Weinstein, *The Corporate Ideal in the Liberal State, 1900–1918* (1968). Murray Rothbard, "War Collectivism in World War I," in *A New History of Leviathan* is very persuasive.

CONCLUSION

In the Progressive era America started becoming the country it is now. As early as the 1890s people were organizing themselves, questioning the principles of laissez-faire and demanding that government meet needs that for many years had not been regarded as government's responsibility. This pressure was exerted locally at first, but during Roosevelt's administration, and even more when Wilson was president, the federal government was obliged to accept new responsibilities. Except briefly during World War I, Washington did not attempt to manage the economy as a whole or to reconcile the interests of every contending interest group. The political events of those years were decisive all the same. In a negative sense the failure of socialism removed any possibility that corporate capitalism might be replaced as the dominant force in economic affairs. The inability of New Nationalists to win support for their program, even in Roosevelt's Progressive party, meant that there would be no master plan for ordering the affairs of the whole nation.

On the other hand, during the Progressive era government committed itself to systematic relations with business and to enhancing the general welfare. It embraced both corporate liberalism and social liberalism. Corporate liberals got the Federal Reserve Act, the Federal Trade Commission, and other measures that had government regulating business, frequently for the sake of businessmen. Social liberals got state laws that regulated the hours and wages of working women and children, and housing, for example, and congressional bills that abolished child labor and protected seamen. In both areas government did not go as far as some progressives, humanitarian reformers especially, wanted it to, while at the same time it went beyond what conservatives thought safe and proper. Yet judging by election returns, until the Great Depression most Americans seemed satisfied with the steps taken to modernize government, meet the needs of major interest groups, and promote social welfare.

When the economy collapsed after 1929 the New Deal's response to it flowed out of the progressive experience. Franklin Roosevelt and other New Dealers had been active progressives, and many New Deal measures were descended from steps taken or advocated in the Progressive era. The National Industrial Recovery Act of 1933 was pure New Nationalism, an attempt at industrial self-regulation under government supervision. The Agricultural Adjustment Act of 1933 was in the line of descent from Wilson's Federal Farm Loan and Warehouse Acts. The National Labor Relations Act of 1935 finally gave unions the protection Gompers had hoped they would gain from the Clayton Act. Many surviving progressives disliked the New Deal precisely because it went beyond what they had advocated in their time. But it was the heir of progressivism all the same, extending the regulatory features of government as New Nationalists had wanted, but also enacting much that social reformers had dreamed of for many years. Yet while the New Deal went beyond progressivism, it operated on many of the same limiting assumptions that governed progressivism. It rejected Socialist solutions to national problems. It favored bargaining over planning. In these respects progressive politics anticipated, and to some extent dictated, the politics of the 1930s and beyond.

The Progressive era also prefigured later developments in nonpolitical areas. Many historians think of the 1920s as the beginning of modern American life. They were the first age of affluence, the age of mass culture, the age of the automobile, a time when the revolution in manners and morals flourished. As we have seen, however, numerous aspects of modern America can be found in the Progressive era. Movies, the first truly mass medium, were entertaining millions of people weekly years before World War I. The flapper was an object of concern as early as 1915. In social terms women were emancipated even before they got the vote. The prosperity of the 1920s was a consequence of productivity gains made earlier. Though a majority of American families did not own automobiles until the 1920s, Henry Ford had begun his mighty work in the previous decade. In 1914 alone he produced nearly a quarter of a million Model T cars.

This is not to say that the society we live in now was formed in the Progressive era. The limited welfare state is an invention of the 1930s. A broadly based consumer culture first appeared in the 1920s. But both of these had roots in the Progressive era, and it seems fair to regard the period as one of transition between the old America of hard work, low incomes, small government, private enterprise, and laissez-faire, and modern America with its forty-hour work week, high wages, lavish consumption, big government, and benevolently regulated enterprise. The Progressive era has often been called an age of reform, and was so regarded at the time, but it is probably more accurate to think of it as an age of modernization. Humanitarians did indeed make certain gains. But the major actions of government in those years were not so much morally uplifting as they were efforts to replace outmoded policies with newer ones appropriate to a complex industrial society comprised of many different and often conflicting interest groups.

As some of these groups had more power than others, all sectors of the population did not benefit equally from modernization. Big businessmen got more than small businessmen, middle-class and professional people more than workers. What were said to be the great evils of the day, political machines and the trusts, suffered little permanent damage. Political organizations pushed out by local reformers generally found ways to get back into government. Few trusts were actually broken up. The Socialist party of Eugene Debs and the antimonopoly campaigns of the Progressive era were perhaps the most severe challenges that corporate capitalism ever faced. By 1920 both had collapsed and the way was clear for big business to go on getting bigger. By 1941, as a result, 1,000 companies controlled 60 percent of the total manufacturing assets of the United States, and by 1968 their number had been further reduced to 200.

The irony of progressive reform as a broadly based effort for democracy and equal opportunity is that, in the end, it helped bring about a different kind of society from what most progressives wanted. If one can speak of a typical progressive, he or she would be a person devoted to competition, direct democracy, community, and a form of government that was small yet responsive. To some extent the typical progressive would favor humanitarian reforms, if they were not too costly, did not require much coercion, and did not seem to perpetuate dependency. But the United States came to be governed by a large, powerful, centralized bureaucracy. The instruments of direct democracy, though available still, have not had much effect on public life. Competition has been greatly reduced by monopolies and oligopolies, governmental favoritism, the influence of special interests upon regulatory agencies, and other devices. If anything, the sense of community has diminished.

Our America is not what progressives had hoped to form for several reasons. They did not anticipate another depression even more severe than that of the 1890s, under circumstances that obliged government to do much more than it ever had before. Most honestly believed that regulation would work well enough to prevent great corporations from achieving the primacy they now enjoy. They failed to appreciate that asserting middle-class claims did not change the fundamental balance of power in society.

The middle-class drive to rationalize and bureaucratize its environment paralleled the attempt of certain big businessmen to achieve the same order and security on the top, enabling capitalists to label as "reforms" measures like the Federal Trade Commission Act that did more for special interests than anyone else. This was not well understood at the time. Almost everyone concerned with public policy in those years was reacting to immediate issues and pressures, and had narrow frames of reference. A few, such as Herbert Croly, and in his own way George Perkins, had some sense of where modernization was taking the country. These were the exceptions. Most who promoted reform did not realize how far some of their initiatives would be carried later, or how ineffective others would prove to be. Despite their sometimes extravagant language, most progressives wanted mainly to close the gap between industrial and urban growth, on the one hand, and government's response to it, on the other. By 1916 or so most appeared to have thought this had been accomplished, hence the failure of Senator La Follette's Progressive party in 1924, hence also the dismay so many old progressives expressed at what seemed to them New Deal excesses in the 1930s. No doubt had they lived longer they would have become even more distressed. The way we live now is partly their doing just the same.

INDEX